REVOLUTION ON EQUATORIA MOUNTAINS

THE STORY OF THE TORIT MUTINY

John Gai Yoh

Copyright © John Gai Yoh
Published by Africa World Books, 2018.
ISBN 978-0-6482591-3-8

Cover design, typesetting and layout: All in One Book Design, Western Australia

All rights reserved. No part of this publication may be reproduced, stored in retrieval system, or transmitted, in any form or by any means without the prior written permission of the author, nor be otherwise circulated in any form of binding or cover other than that in which it is published and without a similar condition being imposed on the subsequent purchaser.

TABLE OF CONTENTS

Dedication	7
Acknowledgements	8
Introduction	10

CHAPTER ONE
The Sudan Defense Force, SDF, 1924-1955 13
 The origins, 13
 The Organization of the SDF, 18
  Recruitment, 21
  Ranking System, 22
  Internal Duties of SDF, 24
  External Duties, 25
  The Sudanization of the SDF, 27
 The Equatorial Corps, 28
  Origins and Formation, 28
End Notes for Chapter One 34

CHAPTER TWO
The Mutiny Of The Equatorial Corps, August 1955 37
 Introduction, 37
 Survey of the events in Torit Town, 41
 The outbreak of the Mutiny, 42
 Implementation of the original Plan, 47
 The Sudan Government Reaction, 54
 The British Government Reaction, 57
 The Egyptian Government Reaction, 61

The Mutiny throughout the South, ?????
The End of the Mutiny, 64
End Notes for Chapter Two   68

CHAPTER THREE
The Causes of the Torit Mutiny   73
 The Commission of Inquiry, 73
 The British Factor, 76
 The Egyptian Connection, 79
 The Communist Element, 82
 The Sudanization Factor, 85
 Al-Azhari government's Attitude, 91
 Psychological Factors, 97
End Notes for Chapter Three   100

CHAPTER FOUR
The Torit Mutiny and its Impact National Politics 105
 The Sudan African National Union (SANU), 114
 The October Uprising, 116
 Challenges of the Southern Organizations, 118
End Notes for Chapter Four   121

CHAPTER FIVE
The Rise and the Development of the Anyanya Movement 124
 The name 'AnyaNya', 126
 Recruitment, 127
  Equatoria Province, 127
  Bahr El Ghazal Province, 128

    Upper Nile Province, 129
    The Propaganda, 133
    The Organizational Structure of the AnyaNya Movement, 134
    Sources of Weaponry, 136
    The Anya Nya Organizational Structure Civil Administration, 138
    The Anya Nya Military and Civilian Organisation, 138
    AnyaNya's Liabilities, 142
    The Birth of the Southern Sudan Liberation Movement (SSLM), 143
End Notes for Chapter Five   148

CHAPTER SIX
Conclusion   151
End Notes for Chapter Six   159

Dedication

Fr Saturnino Lohure
Aggrey Jadden
Joseph Lagu
Samuel Gai Tut
Joseph Oduho
William Deng Nhial
Philip Pedak Lieth
Gordon Mourtat de Mayan
Archanelo Bari Wanji
Ezbone Mondiri Gawnza
Daniel Koat Matthews
George Kwanai

Acknowledgements

The idea of this book was a multi-effort exercise by leading specialists and academics on Sudan to whom, through one of the Middle Eastern experts the late Professor. Albert Hourani, I was introduced. In the early 1990s, Professor Hourani was a visiting scholar with the Department of History at the American University of Beirut, where I was taking a graduate seminar on colonial history of the Middle East. During the seminar Professor Hourani noted that I was interested in geopolitics and the political history of East Africa and Sudan and, as such, he decided to persuade me to write on an original topic, which would deal with some aspects of the British and Egyptian presence in Sudan.

During the same year, late Professor Edward Said, of Columbia University, visited the University and taught a graduate course on Orientalism and made it a point that students interested in colonial history should investigate the origins and the consequences of the colonial decline in Middle East and Africa.

Upon his return to Oxford, Professor Hourani contacted Professors Peter .M Holt, who was in his early 90s at the time, Robert Collins, Gabriel Warburg and Martin Daly, asking them to advise me on what to write. I was gladly surprised to received personal letters from these academic giants, and it was through their advice and the insistence of my academic advisor, Professor Samir Seikaly that I ended up conducting research on the Torit mutiny and its impact on the Sudanese politics.

I am therefore forever grateful to each of those scholars for their valuable advice and their timely intervention. My deep appreciation

Acknowledgements

goes to Professor Seikaly for teaching me the art of academic writing and Professor Kamal Salibi, my lifetime mentor.

I am also grateful to all my colleagues and friends, particularly Dobuony Ruot, Makuach Teny, Zakariah Matur Makuer, John Dak Puok, and Peter Makuoth who encouraged me to publish this work for wider readership. This book was translated into Arabic and published with the same title.

My special thanks goes to Dr Douglas H. Johnson who introduced me to Africa World Books publisher, Peter Deng in Australia. My wife Mary Aban Maluak took the burden of sleepless nights as I worked on the final version of the book, to her and all those who supported me, I extend my appreciation; however, all the shortcomings in the book are solely mine.

Introduction

The history of Torit Munity is a culmination of resistance of the people of Southern Sudan against foreign invasions and foreign interventions in the region. The advent of the Turks, the Egyptians, the British, the French, the Italians, and Belgians in Southern Sudan transition from ethnic cantons to what became Southern Sudan in 1920 can be understood within the context of the formation of the Equatoria Corps in 1924.

The people of Southern Sudan for the first time were recruited into the Sudan army as a separate military unit with headquarters in Torit town, Eastern Equatoria. This book attempts to analyze the origins and evolution of the Revolution on the Equatoria Mountains in August 1955 and the subsequent formation of the Anyanya Movement in December 1963.

The Anyanya Movement, whose political wing later on became the Sudan African National Union (SANU) Movement, was both political and military organization whose main objective was to resist against political, economic, and cultural domination of Northern Sudan.

The Movement was structured in such a way that it decentralized Southern Sudan into three political and military zones: namely Bahr el Ghazal, Equatoria and Upper Nile; although, subsequent disagreements among the leadership of SANU reflected these geographical and demographical divisions of Southern Sudan. While all the leadership of Anyanya and SANU were fully in agreement with the objectives of the struggle, power struggle, counter accusations, and repetitive divisions within the movement

Introduction

leadership, delayed any meaningful negotiations between Southern and Northern leaderships over the status of Southern Sudan.

It took over seventeen years for the two parties to agree on the minimum demand of Southern Sudan: local autonomy. The Addis Ababa Agreement of February 1972 came as a result of unification of different southern Sudan liberation factions under Southern Sudan liberation Movement (SSLM) in 1970, all of whom agreed to support the formation of the SSLM under the leadership of General Joseph Lagu. The quest for Self-determination and Independence by Anyanya Movement and other political movements within the country such as Liberal Party, Southern Front and the Federal Party was put a side in favor of one state two systems under General Jaafar Numeiri.

The Addis Ababa Agreement, due to ideological and political disagreements among Southern Sudanese leaders did not satisfied the separatist group agenda. In March 1975 a group of former Anyanya officers led by Lt. Vincent Kuany Latjor, rebelled in Akobo to be followed in June 1976 by the group of former Anyanya officers in Wau led by Capt. Alfred Awan. In 1977 in Juba International Airport was briefly captured by former Anyanya officers led by Sg. Paul Puok.

All these rebellions culminated in the formation of Anyanya II Movement, which was formed in Ethiopia in 1978 and adopted Self-determination and Independence from the North as their main objective.

Although the activities of Anyanya II were not felt across the country, the military command in Khartoum was worried that the activities of Anyanya II Movement had the potential to destabilize the Upper Nile and Bahr el Ghzal Regions where the Anyanya II recruits were located. It was therefore, not supersizing that in May 1983 when some officers, mainly former Anyanya I Movement, led rebellions in the South and later on joined their colleagues in Anyanya II in Ethiopia to form what became known as the Sudan Peoples Liberation Army and the Sudan People Liberation Movement (SPLA/SPLM).

The main objective of the SPLA/SPLM in fighting Northern Sudan was to resolve what they considered the "Problem of Sudan", in order to achieve the birth of the "New Sudan". As for the separatist tendencies within the SPLM/SPLA, the decision was to use the strategy of dividing Northern Sudanese political establishment in order to achieve the Anyanya One dream of independence and self-determination of people of Southern Sudan

CHAPTER ONE

The Sudan Defense Corps, SDF
1924-1955

The Origins

THE ANGLO-EGYPTIAN ACCORD OF JANUARY 19TH, 1899, OR THE Condominium Agreement, stipulated that military and civilian administrative powers in the Sudan should be vested in a British Governor-General. He was also to be the Commander-in-Chief or *Sirdar* of the Egyptian Army both in the Sudan and in Egypt.[1] The agreement further stipulated that the British garrison in the Sudan and some Egyptian Army units were to be responsible for local security duties. The Governors of the nine provinces into which the Sudan was divided were the British military officers who at the same time were commanding officers of the troops in charge of security in their respective provinces. Although the supreme military commander of the Egyptian army was the Khedive, its actual command was in the hands of the *Sirdar*, who was assisted by two intelligence directors, one in Khartoum and the other in Cairo.[2]

The above hierarchy was constructed in such a way that the Governor-General in his capacity as the Commanding Officer was supposed to be under the authority of the Egyptian Minister of War. This arrangement did not represent a problem as long as Britain enjoyed paramount political influence in Egypt. In fact between 1899 and 1924 all the Egyptian Ministers who held the Ministry of War consented to leave military authority in the hands of the *Sirdar*. The advent, however, of the Wafdist government to power in February 1924, placed the Ministry of War in the hands of a minister who openly announced that all matters concerning the Army had to be referred to him.[4]

Immediately, it became clear that the recognition of Egypt as an independent sovereign state, following the 1922 unilateral declaration of independence, had introduced a new reality into the Anglo-Egyptian political, military and constitutional relations.[5] This new element in Condominium relations made it necessary for the British to find ways and means of establishing complete control over military forces in the Sudan. This goal was to be achieved through the formation of the Sudan Defense Force, SDF.[6]

As a result, the Governor General, Sir Lee Stack, following consultation with the British Foreign Office, submitted in August 1924 a memorandum to the Condominium authorities, in which he proposed a plan for the formation of a Sudan Defense Force.[7] The plan aimed at the replacement of the Egyptian garrison in the Sudan by a force composed exclusively of Sudanese. The new force was to be placed under the Governor-General who should resign his post of *Sirdar* of the Egyptian Army. The Sudan Defense Force, if formed, would take an oath of loyalty, not to the Khedive, but to the Governor-General of the Sudan.[8]

The Sudan Defense Corps, SDF, 1924–1955

While in Cairo negotiating the new proposal with the Egyptian government, Sir Lee Stack was assassinated on 19 November 1924, by a young Egyptian nationalist.[9] On 22 November, Lord Allenby, the British Ambassador to Egypt, delivered an ultimatum to the Egyptian Prime Minister, the Wafd leader Saad Pasha Zaghloul, in which he demanded among other things that:

The Egyptian Government order within 24 hours the withdrawal from the Sudan of all the Egyptian officers and the purely Egyptian units of the Sudan Army with such resulting changes as shall be specified. Failing immediate compliance with these demand(s), His Majesty's Government will at once take appropriate action to safeguard their interests in Egypt.[10]

In a second communiqué containing more specific details Lord Allenby explained:

...The Egyptian officers and purely Egyptian Units of the Egyptian Army having been withdrawn, Sudanese units of the Egyptian Army shall be converted into (a) Sudan Defense Force, owing allegiance to the Sudan Government alone and under Supreme Command of the Governor-General in whose name all commissions will be given.[11]

On the same day of the issuance of the ultimatum, orders were given to the Acting Governor-General of the Sudan for immediate evacuation of Egyptian Army units from the Sudan. In accordance with the terms of the ultimatum, the Acting Governor-General asked the Egyptian units to leave the country within 24 hours.[12] However, on 24th November the Egyptian units in Khartoum North refused to execute the orders they had received, insisting that these orders should come from the Khedive himself. They were surrounded by British troops. On the 27th November six Sudanese officers and two platoons of the 11th Sudanese Battalion, in collaboration with the surrounded Egyptian units in Khartoum North, mutinied.[13]

The British troops tried to negotiate the surrender of the mutineers, but failed to reach a solution and opened fire. The rebels then exchanged fire with the British troops, and stormed the British military hospital killing a British man, two Lebanese medical officers, one non-commissioned officer and three Egyptian soldiers.[14] On 29th November the mutiny was crushed and all the Egyptian units throughout the country were deported. Of the six Sudanese mutinous officers, one turned out to be a government agent; one was killed during the exchange of fire, one was injured and joined the Egyptian troops and the remaining three were sentenced to death. About one hundred soldiers were involved; some surrendered, a few made their way to Khartoum city and caused trouble before they were disarmed. Others fled to Egypt and a few joined their families inside the Sudan.[15]

It is worth pointing out that before the evacuation of the Egyptian Army from the Sudan, the number of the Sudanese troops of the Egyptian Army was about 13,000 men. Beside 106 British officers, there were 233 Sudanese officers.[16]

Once the evacuation of the Egyptian Army was completed, efforts were made to implement Lord Allenby's plan to form the SDF, which was in fact a revised version of Sir Lee Stack's original

The Sudan Defense Corps, SDF, 1924–1955

proposal. By and large, the organization and distribution of the new SDF remained basically unchanged until the mid 1930's. In fact the new Force was organized along the lines of the Egyptian Army, except at the highest levels, where the Commanding Officer was responsible to the Governor-General.[17]

One of the first problems to face the British government was that most of the junior officers in the SDF remained to some extent loyal to King Fu'ad. The Foreign Office had expressed its concern, and urged the Sudanese government to address this question fully and urgently. After consultation with London and Cairo, the Governor-General, Sir Geoffrey Archer, decided that the new SDF should take an oath of allegiance to the Governor-General, rather than to King George; this was of course in conformity with the Anglo-Egyptian Agreement of 1899. The chosen oath for SDF officers and soldiers was as follows:

(I) ... Swear three times by God, by all His Holy Books, by His Apostles, on my conscience and my honour, to be sincerely devoted and faithful to His Excellency the Governor-General of the Sudan, to his Government, and to obey all his orders and all lawful orders which will be given me by my superiors... I further swear that I will faithfully discharge such duties as shall be entrusted to me.[18]

On the King's Day 17th January 1925, Sir Geoffrey Archer, announced the inauguration of the all Sudanese SDF. The creation of the SDF represented therefore complete control of the military in the Sudan by the British government. The title of *Sirdar* became *al-Kaid al-'Amm*,

The first British officer to assume the new post on 11th June 1925 was Colonel Hurbert Hudleston.[19]

The Organization of the SDF

For organizational purposes the Sudan Defense Force was divided into five corps, each corps being a group of three platoons or companies.

The SDF was divided into a Cavalry, a mountain rifles or the Sudan Horse; a Strategic Reserve, an Eastern and Western corps, a Camel corps and an Equatorial Corps.[20] Added to this was a Motor Machine Gun Company composed of three units, two in the capital and one at El-Fasher. Also stationed in the Khartoum area under the Headquarters Command of the SDF were:[21]

An Engineering Corps
It housed the corps' headquarters and was composed of two companies and a Boy Company for training.

The Northern Training Depot
Its assignment was to train the non-commissioned officer instructors both in Rifle and the Motor Machine Gun. It also undertook the training of Native officers.

The Mechanical Transport Department
It was responsible for the provision and the maintenance of all SDF vehicles. It had some subunits in each corps headquarters.

The Sudan Defense Corps, SDF, 1924–1955

The Animal Transport Company-Transport and Supply Unit
It was assigned the responsibility of providing load transport and supplies during patrols or long distance operations.

Stores and Ordinance Department
It provided clothing and equipment required by the SDF, either by purchasing from Britain or by manufacturing them in its own workshops. It is worth mentioning that the SDF also had its own medical corps, which was run by British officers with Syrian medical officers and Sudanese Assistants.

In terms of deployment at the provincial level, the five corps were divided as follows: [22]

Kordufan Province
The headquarters of the Camel Corps was stationed in el-Obeid where two Motorized Infantry Companies were located. There were two corps in Bara; in addition to one Infantry company in Dilling and another in Kadugli.

Kassala Province
Gedaref was designated the headquarters of the Eastern Arab corps where one Infantry company was stationed. One Camel Company was located in Kassala and another one was in Gallabat.

Darfur Province
In El-Fasher, the headquarters of the Western Arab corps, there were one Motorized Machine Gun Battery, one Infantry Company and a Motorized Infantry Company. In Kabkabia district, there

was one Motorized Company; in addition to one Motorized Company in Nyala, there was one Infantry Company in Geneina district.

Shendi (Northern Area)
The Cavalry and the Strategic Reserve were all stationed at Shendi.

The Equatorial Corps
The headquarters of the Equatorial Corps was first stationed at Mongalla, but later moved to Torit district in Eastern Equatoria. There was one Infantry Company in Torit and another in Kapoeta near the Sudan-Kenya border. In addition to one company at Wau, in Bahr El Ghazal Province, there was one company at Tali and another at Aweil. Later on in 1930's several companies were distributed in the Upper Nile Province and in Western Equatoria.

Finally, in terms of numbers the SDF establishment in 1926 consisted of 126 British officers, 41 British non-commissioned officers, 188 Sudanese officers and 7,963 Sudanese soldiers. The provincial distribution was as follows: [23] The Kordufan Province, with stations at al-Obeid, Bara, Talodi, Kadugli and Dilling had 1,700 troops. In the Northern Province, over 1,500 troops were stationed in the three towns of (Khartoum, Khartoum North and Umdurman) as well as Shendi. In Darfur Province, over 1,100 troops were posted at al-Fasher, Kabkabia and Geneina. In Kassala Province, there were over a thousand at Gedaref, Kassalla, and Singa Abdulla. The Equatorial Corps, which was composed of ten companies, remained stationed in the South; it consisted of about three hundred men. It was, however, subjected to different terms of recruitment, regulation and pay.

Every company of SDF was housed in a fort, a collection of buildings surrounded by barbed wire and an inner wall. The fort served as the company headquarters. In other words, it was the defensive area in which the whole company could be protected.[24] Each fortress comprised a guardroom, the company main office, the office of the company accountant and the office of the civilian interpreter. The later individual was important to the company, especially in those areas where the commander of the corps was not well versed in the local languages. Adjacent to the fortress was the company stores. Next to the guardroom were the two flags, the Union Jack and the Egyptian lag, representing the Condominium?

The company commander was responsible for recruitment and the training of his men and was the final authority in his corps. He also had to see to it that the morale and the readiness of his troops was at high level.[25]

Recruitment

It was the policy of the SDF that each company had to carry out its own recruitment. This policy seems to suggest that the majority of recruits in a particular company, if not all of them, came from the same area. Since the pay of the SDF soldiers was low, two Sudanese pounds and a hundred piasters (2.100) per month for a new recruit, recruitment was voluntary. In general, the new recruit signed on for nine years, renewable for up to eighteen years.[26]

The training procedures for both officers and NCOs of the SDF, was based on the British model. Sudanese officers were sent to

Britain, Pakistan, India and Egypt for advanced training. In principle, the Training College offered a two-year course leading to a commission as a second Lieutenant in the Army. Graduates were temporarily placed on probation for two years before receiving their permanent commissions as first Lieutenants, a practice that is followed up to the present.[27]

The selection of candidates for the Sudanese officer corps was based on merit, candidates from the nine provinces were entitled to apply; but those from the three Southern provinces were admitted to the College only if they possessed perfect knowledge of Arabic, a requirement, which often disadvantaged many who qualified for admission.

In practice, a candidate should be physically fit, unmarried, Sudanese under (21) years of age if he was a secondary school graduate, and under (25) if a university student. The training of the NCOs and the officer corps was carried out by British warrant officers; they were seconded to the SDF headquarters for this assignment.[28]

Ranking System

The highest rank in the SDF was that of Lieutenant General, the equivalent of *Ferik* in Arabic/Turkish usage.[29] Each company of SDF, a sub-unit of about (100-150) men, was commanded by a British major. It is worth mentioning out that all the SDF titles were of Turkish origin, a legacy of the Egyptian Army, Egypt being historically part of the Ottoman Empire.

Therefore, O*nmbashi* was equivalent to corporal, *Shawish*-sergeant; *Bash Shawish* - sergeant major; *Mulazim*-Lieutenant; *Yuzbashi* - Captain; *Sagholash* - between Captain and Major; *Bimbashi* - major,

The Sudan Defense Corps, SDF, 1924–1955

Kaimakam - Lt. Colonel; *Miralai* - Colonel; *Liwa* - Brigadier and *Ferik* - Major General.[30]

While Lt. Colonel and Colonel carried the title of B*ey*, both Brigadier and Major General carried the title of P*asha.* The lowliest post held by the British officers serving in Sudan was that of major.

The Sudanese officers or the 'Native officers' as they were called, acted as assistants to the British officers in charge of the company. It was a necessity that a native officer be attached to a British officer to inform him about the background of the troops, their ethnic origins, their customs and their habits.[31] Most often the majority of the Native officers came from the upper and to some extent the middle classes of the towns. For promotion purposes all officers were required to sit for examinations, which ensured that the higher ranks were filled with competent and qualified personnel.

The pay of the officers was sufficient to provide them with a comfortable standard of living.[32] The SDF stores and Ordinance Department provided military uniforms to the troops, which resembled those of British Army. However, some transformations were introduced for climatic differences. Furthermore, clothing varied from North to South. For instance, shorts and leg wear were issued for the soldiers in the North, while long trousers were worn in the South.

The code of military law used by the SDF was that to which the Egyptian Army had been subjected before the formation of the SDF. Based on the India Codes of Military Law, the SDF codes were therefore similar to the British Military Law, although there were some minor differences. The SDF's company commander had, for instance, the authority to promote or to demote and could detain a soldier up to (25) days. However, in cases where the company commander could not decide, he had to refer the case to the Commanding Officer of the corps.[33]

The Internal Duties of SDF

One of the main problems that faced the SDF units was the distance problem. In a country as vast as the Sudan, it was very difficult for the headquarters in Khartoum to control all the SDF units. Thus, it was necessary for each company to rely on itself.[34] This meant in practice that the army had to supply their own provisions and quarters; all the government could do was to supply them with salaries, clothing and furniture. It was only while on active patrols or on operations that they were provided with rations, most of the time in the form of *durra* (wheat) flour.

There was no permanent mess in each company; single soldiers were however, housed in a barrack-room in the fortress.[35] It is noted that it was the Sudan government's intention that the role of the SDF would be purely the maintenance of internal security, since no one envisaged any outside threat, at least, before World War II. It was intended that such a role would require only the use of one company or at most two in one operation. Therefore, such a force would only require minimal communications (i.e. camels, horses) and the medical service of one doctor. Thus, between 1925 and 1930, the SDF was engaged in internal security operations or patrols. These patrols were carried out against ethnic communities, which refused to submit to government authority. These minor operations were undertaken with the consent of and in cooperation with the District Commissioner (DC) of the area concerned.[36]

During 1920's and because there was lack of fast roads, much of the patrols were carried out on foot. Another task of the SDF companies was the 'show of the Flag'. This job required each company to walk several hundred miles, which lasted sometimes several weeks. The aim of these "Flag Shows" was to extend the government authority in those areas, which remained un-pacified, especially in the three Southern provinces. [37]

External Duties

The Italian invasion of Eritrea and Ethiopia in 1935, created a new major threat to British interests in East Africa. This new threat prompted the SDF commander Major General Harold Franklyn to introduce new reforms in the SDF. It was General Franklyn's belief that for the SDF to be transformed into a fighting force, it was necessary that some SDF companies be strengthened. This meant that Camel companies and Motorized Infantry had to be converted into six Motor Machine Gun companies. Each company consisted of an armoured car platoon, a light van platoon and three Infantry platoons in troop-carrying vehicles. The Sudan Service Corps and the Sudan Signals were also formed. When Major General William Platt took over as the SDF Commanding officer in 1939, he introduced Artillery and anti-tanks guns into the SDF armoury.[38] In addition to the above steps, the following companies were introduced:[39]

The Frontier Battalion

It was an Infantry Battalion consisting of five companies. Its task was to pave the way for Emperor Haile Sallasie's return to Addis Ababa. This Battalion was commanded by Miralai Hugh Boustead Bey.

The Composite Battalion
It was composed of four Infantry companies; its officer corps consisted of a British and a Sudanese officer. It was charged with reinforcing Frontiers posts. It was commanded by Miralai J. Gifford Bey.

The Equatorial Corps
Its assignment was to patrol the Eastern Frontier of Southern Sudan. It was commanded by Miralai F.O. Cave Bey.

When Italy declared war in June 1940, the Sudan government realized that it had to face 300,000 Italians with a force of less than 6,000 SDF troops. Efforts were made to recruit additional Sudanese for the SDF, especially in the South. In February 1941 the SDF was opened to Armenians, Lebanese, Greeks and Syrians residing in the Sudan.[40] The SDF was also put under a wider command which covered North and East Africa, and which had bases as far as Cairo, Khartoum and Nairobi. General William Platt became, in addition to his post as Commander-in-Chief of SDF, the General Officer Commanding troops in the Sudan.[41] The task of the SDF during the war was to watch, harass and if possible delay the enemy until reinforcements of British Imperial Forces could arrive.

It continued to patrol the borders as well as collecting intelligence information about the enemy. When reinforcements did

The Sudan Defense Corps, SDF, 1924–1955

arrive, some SDF units were reassigned other tasks such as recapturing some areas in North Africa. However, the entrance of the SDF into Addis Ababa on 5th May 1941 with the invading British troops raised many questions over its status beyond the Sudan borders. Since the SDF had no charter, British authorities ruled that its sphere of operations was unlimited.

The SDF presence in Eritrea was also justified as an extension of its normal service in defending the Sudan. The same arguments were later used in the case of the SDF involvement in Libya.[42] It is worth mentioning that after 1940, the SDF was placed under British War Office control. By the end of the war in 1945 the strength of SDF had reached about 25,000 native troops and it returned to its original role of internal security. From 1945 on, demobilization process began until the number of the force fell to 7,750 in 1947.[43]

The Sudanization of the SDF

The last British officer to hold the post of the SDF *Kaid Al-Amm* was Major General Reginald L. Scoones. In a report to the Military Advisory Committee of the Sudanization Commission in June 1954, General Scoones reported that the authorized establishment of the SDF was 215 British and Sudanese officers. In the same report he pointed out that, whereas Sudanization would work easily in the North, the removal of the British officers from the Southern corps would be a dangerous and unwise move.[44] In one of the committee's meetings, General Scoones was quoted as warning the committee members "not to try to do it (Sudanize) all in one and on no account to hurry the South."[45] However, despite General Scoones warnings, the Council of Ministers decided in May 1954, that SDF should be

27

Sudanized as of June of the same year. This actually meant that the remaining British officers serving with the SDF should leave the Sudan by July 1954 the *Kaid Al-Amm* would leave by August 1955. The Sudanization of the SDF did not pose any problem in the North, where the Sudanese majors easily filled British posts in the Camel, Eastern and Western Arab corps.[46]

Unlike the North, and for political reasons, government policy in the South had been to have only British officers serving with the Equatorial corps. However, this policy, which was abandoned in June 1954, led to many political repercussions as shall be discussed later. In August 1954, the first Sudanese officer, *Liwa* Ahmed Pasha Mohammed, was appointed as *al-Kaid Al-Amm* to replace the British officer, General Scoones.[47]

The Equatorial Corps

Origins and Formation

The idea of forming a Southern corps of Anglo-Egyptian Army was motivated by two main reasons: The constant British fear of Islamic penetration into Southern Sudan; and the difficulties faced by the Anglo-Egyptian military command in recruiting soldiers among Southern Sudanese communities. In a letter to R.C.R. Owen, the Governor of Mongalla Province, the Governor-General Rignald Wingate Pasha, on December 1910, asked the former, among other things, to present a plan through which Southern recruits into Anglo-Egyptian Army could be increased.[48] Governor Owen proposed instead what amounted

The Sudan Defense Corps, SDF, 1924-1955

to a new model of Army for the South. He suggested a new force, recruited purely among Southerners, officially Christian, have English as its Service Language and whose officers would be British.[49]

In addition, and in accordance with the administrative regulations of 1910, it was stated that the Sudanese of the following classes should be taken for recruitment: runaway servants who refuse to return to their masters; servants who refuse to work or who were liable to persecution as idle persons; those without permanent employment who may be charged with minor offences and those boys in towns without occupation can also be enlisted provided that they were medically fit.[50]

Indeed, it was among these Southern groups that the government could easily find recruits. Moreover, since recruitment was resented by most Southern ethnicities, the government made it a point to pay bounties to volunteers and to recruiting agents, government administrators, non-commissioned officers and soldiers who brought in a recruit.[51]

In fact, Governor-General Wingate Pasha had often blame the Southern Sudanese reluctance to recruit into the Anglo-Egyptian Army and considered it as a result of their anti-apathy towards Islam. The Anglo-Egyptian Army was 95% Muslim and Southern Sudanese who were recruited prior to 1910 regulations, were, if not already nominally Muslims, almost always converted. That was why Wingate Pasha had considered the system of turning all Southern recruits into Muslims, to be behind the lack of recruits in Southern region.[52] He suggested; as a result

'A Territorial System' to ensure that recruits remained nearer home, which was a perfect solution to Southern Sudanese recruits. It would also give the government:

The opportunity of getting rid of the moslimising influence in the shape of Egyptian officers and fanatical Sudanese N.C.O.s, and very gradually dropping the Moslem conditions in all Sudanese Battalions of the Anglo-Egyptian Army[53]

Indeed Wingate's suggestion had matched with Governor Owen's view that the new Southern corps would be part of what he considered to be a comprehensive Southern policy, aiming at creating:

… A large Christian population which would eventually link up with Uganda and form a substantial buffer or check to the spread of Islam, which may at any time break out into a wave of fanaticism.[54]

However, despite his approval of the plan in principle, the idea of a purely Christian army in the South was too much for Wingate Pasha. After all, he had never contemplated detaching Southern Sudan from his authority, let alone linking it up with Uganda. Although hesitant, Wingate Pasha welcomed Owen's proposal.[55]

In addition to the above arguments, there were also other factors that necessitated the formation of Equatorial Corps, as the Southern Battalion became known; troops raised locally would be cheaper; they could be paid, fed and clothed according to local recruitment, not up to Egyptian Army standards. Furthermore,

The Sudan Defense Corps, SDF, 1924–1955

they would speak the language of the district in which they were stationed and knew the country better than outsiders. The Equatorial corps was assigned the work to man the outposts, while small striking force of regular soldiers would remain at province headquarters at Mongalla.[56]

Governor Owen's original plan called for three companies, one in the Bahr el-Ghazal the others in Mongulla, leading eventually to six companies, two in Bahr-El-Ghazal and four in Mongalla. It was the government view that those enlisted would suffice for the region where, in any case, there was no enemy of importance. The basic problem was the difficulty of obtaining suitable British officers. Governor-General Wingate Pasha decided that the only suitable solution to the problem was to commission officers to the South.[57] Thus, the formation of a Southern Corps was officially approved in 1911 and recruitment among Southern communities started immediately.

By January 1914, the first Operational Company of the Equatorial Corps was able to take over the 12th Sudanese Company at Yambio in Western Equatoria and in 1915 another company took over at Tambura. In the same year the government administrators in the South were notified that: "in accordance with Belgian and Uganda traditions, Sunday and not Friday is to be the holiday in your district."[58] On 7th December 1917, the Equatorial Corps took over the security task in Mongalla, and on 3rd January 1918, Governor Owen was able to inform the Governor-General that Sunday was now the official holiday throughout his province and that the Equatorial Corps has controlled the whole province.

The replacement of the Anglo-Egyptian Army garrisons by the

Equatorial Corps and the introduction of Sunday holiday were gradually accomplished in Bahr El-Ghazal province in 1920's.[59]

The Governor of Bahr El-Ghazal, L.F. Nalder, noted in 1926 that the deployment of the Equatorial Corps in his province "Would be a step in the work of spreading Christianity in the province and would be of course welcomed by the Christian missionary societies and American Presbyterian Mission."[60] In 1927 a company of Equatorial Corps was posted to Upper Nile province.

As discussed earlier the Sudanization of the SDF was carried out in the North without difficulties. The situation in the South was however, different. In January 1954, there were (10) British officers in the Equatorial Corps, including the Commanding Officer Lt. Colonel W.B.E. Brown.[61] In addition to Infantry, there were the Service Corps, the Engineers, Signals and the Boys Company. The order to Sudanize the British posts in the Equatorial Corps was received in the middle of June 1954. Five weeks later the corps was handed over and on 29th July the outgoing Commanding Officer and his British colleagues sailed to Khartoum.[62]

On the eve of the independence, the Equatorial Corps was ethnically dominated by Equatoria communities mainly from Acholi, Bari, Lotuka, Zande and Madi. Only about hundred of them were from Nilotes ethnic groups-the Nuer, Dinka, Shilluk etc. By the end of 1955, the majority of the army and police officers were from Northern Sudan. For instance, of the 33 officers in the Equatorial Corps, the 24 seniors were Northerners, and only (9) junior officers* were Southerners. The proportion was much the same in the police and the civil administration. The headquarters of the Southern Corps was based in the town of Torit in Eastern Equatoria.[63]

The Sudan Defense Corps, SDF, 1924–1955

On the whole, before independence it was generally held that the Sudanese army officers in all the SDF corps were not interested in politics. However, as the British departure approached, many officers became outspoken about political issues.[64] In fact, when the coup leaders in Egypt declared their country a republic in July 1953, some officers in the SDF tried to organize military coups in the Sudan. At that time the Northern Sudanese officer corps was split, one faction being in favour of merging with Egypt and the other wanting complete independence.

In the South the situation was even more delicate, especially after the November 1953 elections. The promises made by the Northern political parties during the election campaigns, i.e. to consider Southern political, administrative and economic demands, were not fulfilled. Fears of potential persecution by the Northern dominated government after the British departure began to take shape in the South. The Equatorial Corps, particularly the Southern Officer Corps, began to become involved in politics, in collaboration with the Southern Liberal Party-the only Southern Political Party at the time.[65]

When orders were issued that some Southern units of the Equatorial Corps go to Khartoum to attend the farewell parade of the Condominium troops, the whole Southern Corps rejected the orders and mutinied on 18th August 1955; first in the town of Torit, then all over the big towns in the South. The description of the Mutiny, the causes behind it, and its political repercussions will be the subject of discussions below.

End Notes

1. The full text of Anglo-Egyptian Agreement of January 1899 is found in Muddathir Abd al-Rahim, *Imperialism and Nationalism* (London: The Clarendon Press, 1969), pp. 229-235; also see Martin W. Daly, *Empire on the Nile: The Anglo-Egyptian Sudan, 1898-1934* (Cambridge: Cambridge University Press, 1991), pp. 14-18; also see M.I. Abdulla, "The External and Internal Roles of the Sudan Defense Force," in *The Condominium Remembered: The Making of the Sudan State*, vol. 1, (Durham: University of Durham, 1991), pp. 135-140.

2. Sir Harold Mac Michael, *The Anglo-Egyptian Sudan*, (London: Faber and Faber, Ltd., 1934), pp. 149-163; Daly, *Empire on the Nile*, pp. 88-93.

3. Mac Michael, *The Anglo-Egyptian Sudan*, pp. 159-163.

4. J.S.R. Ducan, *The Sudan: A Record of Achievement* (London: William Blackwood and Sons Ltd., 1952), pp. 139-42.

5. Ibid., pp. 139-41.

6. Robert O. Collins, *Shadows in the Grass: Britain in the Southern Sudan, 1918-1956* (New Haven: Yale University Press, 1983), pp. 65-71.

7. Pierre Crabites, *The Winning of the Sudan* (London: George Routledge and Sons, Ltd., 1934), pp. 189-197.

8. Ducan, *The Sudan*, pp. 137-142.

9. Peter Woodward, *Sudan 1898-1989: The Unstable State* (London: Lester Crook Academic Publishing, 1990), pp. 42-44; Ducan, *The Sudan*, pp. 136-140.

10. Mac Michael, *The Anglo-Egyptian Sudan*, pp. 154-63; Sir Harold Mac Michael, *The Sudan*, (London: Ernest Benn, Ltd., 1954), pp. 181-199.

11. Ducan, *The Sudan*, pp. 135-142.

12. Crabites, *The Winning of the Sudan*, pp. 189-197.

13. Peter M. Holt and Martin W. Daly, *A History of the Sudan: From Coming of Islam to the Present Day*, 4th ed. (London: Longman, 1988), pp. 133-35; Also see Collins, *Shadows in the Grass*, pp. 64-70.

14. *US Army Area Handbook for the Republic of the Sudan*, 2nd ed., (Washington D.C., The American University, 1964), pp. 457-472.

15. Ibid., pp. 460-472.

16. Abdulla, "External and Internal Roles of the Sudan Defense Force", p. 137.

17. Daly, *Empire on the Nile*, pp. 305-322.

18. Ibid., pp. 304-323.

The Sudan Defense Corps, SDF, 1924-1955

19 Collins, *Shadows in the Grass,* pp. 80-82.
20 Edgar O'Ballance, *The Secret War in the Sudan, 1955-1972* (Connecticut: Archon Books, 1977), pp. 38-43; also see Col. J.H.R. Orlebar, "The Story of the Sudan Defense Force 1925-1955", in *The Condominium Remembered: The Making of the Sudanese State,* Vol. 1, (Durham: University of Durham, 1911), pp. 99-106.
21 Daly, *Empire on the Nile,* pp. 322-23; also Orlebar, "The Story of the Sudan Defense Force", p. 105.
22 See Orlebar, "The Story of the Sudan Defense Force," p. 106.
23 Daly, *Empire on the Nile,* pp. 322-325.
24 Orlebar, "The Story of the Sudan Defense Force", p. 101.
25 Ibid., p. 102.
26 *US Army Handbook For the Republic of the Sudan,* pp. 457-472.
27 Ibid., pp. 458-460.
28 See Orlebar, "The Story of the Sudan Defense Force, p. 104.29 *US Army Handbook for the Republic of the Sudan,* pp. 451-470.
30 Orlebar, "The Story of the Sudan Defense Force", p. 103.
31 Ibid., pp. 102-116.
32 *US Army Area Handbook----,* pp. 460-72.
33 Ibid., pp. 451-470.
34 Orlebar, "The Story of the Sudan Defense Force", pp. 100-102.
35 Ibid., p. 101.
36 Ibid., pp. 106-132.
37 See K.D.D. Henderson, *Sudan Republic* (London: Ernest Benn Ltd., 1965), pp. 156-164.
38 Martin W. Daly, *Imperial Sudan: The Anglo-Egyptian Condominium, 1934-1956* (Cambridge: Cambridge University Press, 1991), pp. 127-134.
39 Orlebar, "The Story of the Sudan Defense Force", pp. 115-116.
40 Daly, *Imperial Sudan,* pp. 127-140.
41 Ibid., pp. 135-141
42 Ibid., p. 135.
43 Abdalla, "External and Internal Roles of the Sudan Defense Force", pp. 139-142.
44 Ibid., p. 140.
45 See Orlebar, "The Story of the Sudan Defense Force", p. 134.
46 Oliver Albino, *The Sudan: A Southern Viewpoint* (London: Oxford University Press, 1970), pp. 31-36.

47 Abdalla, "External and Internal Roles of the Sudan Defense Force", p. 140.
48 Details are given by Lilian P. Sanderson and Neville Sanderson, *Education, Religion and Politics in Southern Sudan, 1899-1964* (London: Ethaca Press, 1981), 81-95; also see Daly, *Empire on the Nile*, pp. 114-116.
49 See Daly, *Empire on the Nile*, pp. 133-151.
50 Sanderson, *Education, Religion and Politics in Southern Sudan*, pp. 82-83; see Daly, *Empire on the Nile*, p. 115.
51 Sanderson, *Education, Religion and Politics in Southern Sudan*, p. 83; also see Daly, *Empire on the Nile*, pp. 115-117.
52 See Daly, *Empire on the Nile*, pp. 115-116.
53 Sanderson, *Education, Religions, Politics in Southern Sudan*, pp. 84-87; Daly, *Empire on the Nile*, p. 116.
54 Sanderson, *Education, Religion and Politics---*, p. 83.
55 Mohammed O. Beshir, *The Southern Sudan: Background to Conflict* (Khartoum: University of Khartoum Press, 1968), pp. 36-47.
56 Daly, *Empire on the Nile*, pp. 117-188.
57 Ibid., p. 117.
58 Sanderson, *Education, Religion and Politics in Southern Sudan*, p. 84.
59 Ibid., p. 85.
60 Ibid., pp. 85-87.
61 W.B.C. Brown, "Some Reminiscences and Personal Views Concerning the Sudanization of the Equatorial corps, SDF, in 1954," in *The Condominium Remembered: The Making of the Sudanese State*, vol. 1, (Durham: University of Durham, 1991), pp. 141-143.
62 Woodward, *Sudan, 1898-1989*, pp. 88-91.
63 Dustan M. Wai, *The African-Arab Conflict in the Sudan* (New York: Africana Publishing Company, 1981), pp. 64-68; also see Takrir Lajnat Tahkik al-Idari fi Hawadith al Junub as-Sudan, (Khartoum: October 1956), pp. 27-36; on the Sudanization of the Equatorial Corps see Brown "Some Reminiscences and Personal Views Concerning the Sudanization of the Equatorial Corps", pp. 142-143. * The names, ranks and tribal origins of these officers were difficult to be traced; however, they might be found in the SDF files.
64 Daly, *Imperial Sudan*, pp. 382-394.
65 Henderson, *Sudan Republic*, pp. 61.

CHAPTER TWO

The Mutiny of the Equatorial Corps
August 1955

Introduction

THE BRITISH PRESENCE IN THE SOUTHERN SUDAN WAS CONSIDERED BY MANY Southerners as the only means for the effective protection of Southern interests in Sudan. Indeed, it was widely believed that once the British left the Sudan, the Southern fears of a possible Northern domination would become a reality.[1] Perhaps as a kind of confirmation of this fear, when the British departure from the Sudan approached, several Northern government officials in the South petitioned the central government to restate Sudanese troops in order to increase the number of Northern soldiers in to the South. Their petitions, were to some extent caused by the already deteriorating relationship between them and their Southern counterparts in the military as well as civil government institutions in the region.[2]

The Commander of the Sudan Defense Force turned down these requests on the ground that such action would represent a kind of provocation directed against the Southern troops of the SDF,

37

although he was confident that the Southern Battalion, which was scheduled to leave for Khartoum in order to participate in the farewell ceremonies would obey his orders. Thus, he ordered Company No. 2 of the Equatorial Corps to leave Torit for Juba and from there to Khartoum.[3]

One week later, in the course of an investigation relating to an attempt on the life of the Acting Commander of the Equatorial Corps, it became apparent that a plot to mutiny was being hatched in the Southern corps of the SDF. The interrogation revealed that the accused, Corporal Saturlino Oboya, was an active member of the Southern Liberal Party* who had been apparently warned by his party about the possibility of troop transfers.[4]

The investigation also revealed that the accused had mobilized a considerable number of Southern officers against such a move. Documents linking him and some officers and soldiers to other Southern garrisons were also found.[5] They showed that Corporal Saturlino using his position as the corps telegraph operator, had contacted the garrisons in Malakal, Juba and Wau; encouraging insubordination among the Southern corps in the three Southern provinces.

Upon receiving the final report of the investigation, the Juba District Commissioner ordered the arrest of two government officials, Marco Effendi Rume and Daniel Effendi Jume both of whom where members of the Southern Liberal Party, and who seem to have been aware of Saturlino's intention to provoke an uprising.[6] On the following day August 9th, a crowd of about 600 to 800 people gathered around Juba prison demanding the release of the two Southerners. The Juba District Commissioner, Mr. Mohammed

The Mutiny of the Equatorial Corps, August 1955

Abdel Karim called upon two Equatoria elders, Yasia Lokiri, a member of Senate, and Chief Lolik Lado to convince the crowd to stop their demonstration, emphasizing the seriousness of the crime in which the two officials were involved. However, the crowd refused to talk to the two elders, and requested, instead, to talk to the District Commissioner (DC) personally. Unwilling to address the angry crowd, the DC ordered the police to fire tear gas instead. As a result the demonstrators dispersed, but none of them were arrested.[7]

The Commander of the Equatoria Corps, who was on leave in Khartoum, arrived on August 9th in Juba and chaired a security meeting in the province's headquarters. The meeting was attended by the Equatoria Commissioner, the Juba District Commissioner, the Equatoria Police Chief, Commissioner of Bahr el-Ghazal, Mr. Daud Abdel Latif, and Colonel Arwa Pasha, former Assistant Commander of the Equatorial Corps. Having assessed and discussed the situation at length, the meeting resolved that it was important to bring army reinforcements from the North, that none of the troops implicated in the plot would be arrested until all preparations were completed and that the two civilians implicated in the conspiracy would remain under arrest.[8]

As mentioned earlier, the investigation had revealed that corporal Saturlino Oboya had established contacts with other Southern officers among them Lieutenant Reynaldo Loyola. On August 4th, 1955, for instance, Saturlino had wired Reynaldo informing him that 'trouble' would break out the next day (August 5th) at 5:00 p.m. in Torit and asked him to carry out similar disturbances in Juba. He further asked Reynaldo to send two platoons to Mongalla on

August 5th, in order to confront the Northern Army coming from the North. On August 5th Saturlino had sent yet another message to Reynaldo reaffirming what he had said the day before, and adding that Reynaldo must occupy the airport and must assume personal command of battalions going to Mongalla Station, and must arrange for the transfer of battalion stationed at Yambio to join him.9

On August 6th Reynaldo responded to Saturlino messages, assuring him that there were no grounds for his misgivings and urging him not to become involved in any mutiny whatsoever.[10] He was keen in avoiding any move that may reveal the plot at its early stages.

On the same day, Saturlino Oboya sent a message, through Lieutenant Reynaldo, to Marco Effendi Rume, the Secretary of the Liberal Party committee in Juba. In the message, he informed Rume of his inability to convince the officers and soldiers in Torit to mutiny. He told Rume that he had resigned from his post as a Chairman of the Southern Corps, as of August 5th, 1955.[11]

In another message, which was supposed to have been sent on the same day, Saturlino repeated his previous message to Rume and regretted his inability to proceed with his plan in an uprising. Saturlino said in his message that he had summoned his colleagues in the Equatoria Corps in Torit, and told them about the arrangements regarding the transfer of Northern Sudanese army to the South, and added that his explanation did not convince his colleagues. Instead, his colleagues told him to wait for the arrival of Both Diu, the Secretary General of the Southern Liberal Party from Khartoum, after which the Corps would decide what to do.

The Mutiny of the Equatorial Corps, August 1955

In this message Saturlino seemed bitter because Marco had "failed to provide him with adequate information concerning anything that would make him happy", as he put it.[12] In fact, Saturlino's failure to start a mutiny seemed to have disillusioned him to the point of desperation. Unprepared and rashly, he attempted to assassinate the Acting Commander of the Equatoria Corps. This incident led to the discovery of the whole plot. Saturlino was arrested on August 6th, but escaped or was released later when the mutiny did actually take place on August 18th, 1955.[13]

Survey of the Events in Torit Town

On 17th August a second security meeting was held at the Equatoria provincial headquarters in Juba. In that meeting several suggestions were made to reduce existing tensions in the region. Some of the suggestions included a proposal for the destruction of all ammunition depots at Torit by Northern Sudanese officers in the Equatorial Corps. The Commanding Officer rejected this proposal arguing that such action would incite the soldiers to start a mutiny even if they had not thought of it. The meeting instead, resolved that No. 2 Company of the Equatoria Corps, stationed in Torit, must, for the prestige and dignity of the army, proceed to Khartoum as scheduled earlier.[14] Similar orders were issued to company No. 5 of the Southern Corps at Malakal. The meeting also decided to recommend that additional Northern forces be airlifted to the South.[15] Northern soldiers in Torit, had in the meantime begun to evacuate their families. This move added to the widely circulating rumors that Southern troops would be mistreated upon arrival in Khartoum. The official statement provided by the government concerning the transfer of the two Southern companies to the North, was that they would participate in the farewell parade of colonial troops in Khartoum.

Not convinced by the above explanation, the troops of the Equatoria Corps disobeyed the orders to get into the waiting lorries to take them from Torit to Juba. Their rejection led to a mutiny on 18th August 1955.[16]

Prior to the departure for the parade on 18th August the Commanding Officer Ismail Pasha Salim, had as a precautionary move, ordered that only guns without ammunition would be distributed to each platoon; once the platoon received its arms, it would get into the waiting lorries and proceed directly to Juba on its way to Khartoum.

The Outbreak of the Mutiny

At 7:30 a.m. on 18th August, company No. 2 of the Equatorial Corps, was assembled on the parade ground, adjacent to a building, which served as the headquarters of the Corps in Torit. At the parade there were five Northern Sudanese officers: Colonel Ismail Pasha Salim, the Commanding Officer of the Corps, Major Mahjoub Taha, Captain Banaga Abdel Hafiz, Captain Salah Abdel Majid, and Lieutenant Mohammed Abdel Kadir. Lieutenant Hussein Ahmed Khalifa was waiting in the arms store to deliver arms to each platoon upon its arrival. The remaining eight Northern officers and two corporals

The Mutiny of the Equatorial Corps, August 1955

were in their offices or on other assignments. The Boys platoon were playing in the football ground with their commander, Captain Hasan Fahl.[17]

The mutiny started at 7:45 a.m. when the first platoon was ordered to proceed from parade ground to arms depot under the command of sergeant Mathiang. The platoon marched smartly, passed by the Commanding Officer and gave him the salute in the usual manner. Suddenly, a murmur was heard among the soldiers in the rest of the company. The First Platoon received their rifles and then hurried to return to the company, refusing to stand at attention. No. 2 Company immediately rushed to the arms store, seized the arms and ammunition and deserted the parade yard.[18]

Upon the return of the First platoon Captain Salah Abdel Majid rushed toward Sergeant Mathiang and ordered him to go directly to the lorries with his platoon. Mathiang replied that his platoon would like to talk with Colonel Salim concerning the length of their stay in Khartoum. In the meantime soldiers of the First Platoon began to shoot randomly at their Northern colleagues and disorder ensued in the barracks. Almost at the same time, Colonel Salim, who was at a distance from Platoon No. 2, ordered Lieutenant Mohammed Abdel Kadir to inform Sergeant Mathiang and the rest of platoons that the Commander of the Corps had decided that the journey to Juba would be indefinitely postponed. Unable to reach the platoons because of the random shooting and disorder, Lieutenant Mohammed went directly to inform Captain Hasan Fahl and his boys about the mutiny.[19]

At this stage the Commanding Officer, having failed to reach the arms depot, decided to drive to the district headquarters using the Torit airport road. Major Banaga Abdel Hafiz and Captain Salah, who were accompanying him, were instantly killed in cross fire. Upon his arrival at the district headquarters, the Commanding Officer briefed the Assistant District Commissioner Barnaba Effendi. They agreed that the situation had deteriorated considerably, and that it was necessary that the remaining Northern officers should leave the city. While the meeting was in progress, a group of mutineers arrived, and attempted to fire at Colonel Salim. The mutineers were eventually disarmed by the police who were still loyal to the Assistant District Commissioner, himself a Southerner. Arrangements were made, and Colonel Salim, Major Mahjoub Taha and the Police Chief, a Southerner, managed to escape and arrived at Kateri Station at about 10:45 a.m.[20]

Having controlled the arms and ammunition stores, the mutineers began a general hunt down of Northern Sudanese officers, soldiers and others who were unsuccessfully trying to escape. By about 9:30 a.m. the mutiny became known to almost everyone in the city. The city residents were armed and along with the rebels started robbing Northern properties. Meanwhile most of the mutineers spent the whole day of 18th August evacuating their families; on the same day many residents left the city to the nearby villages because of the fighting and about 53 civilians drowned while trying to cross Kiniti river running outside the town.

In the evening, all the Northern Sudanese survivors gathered in two houses, sending some of their children to spend the night in the Catholic mission.[21] On the same day, about 190 troops mutinied in Juba, Yei, Yambio and Maridi, of whom 138 tried to coordinate with the original mutineers in Torit, by crossing into

The Mutiny of the Equatorial Corps, August 1955

Uganda with the intention of re-crossing into the Sudan near Torit.[22] They were however disarmed by the Ugandan authorities. The other 52 remained in the bushes of Western Equatoria.[23]

On 19th August, robbery of the Northern Sudanese shops continued. Upon police request all the Northern Sudanese in the town were assembled in the district prison. Having learned about this move, the mutineers rushed to the prison and asked the police Sergeant in charge to give them the keys of the prison. The Sergeant rejected their request. Late in that evening, Lieutenant Reynaldo Loyola and Lieutenant Mundiri Ozaki arrived in Torit, following their successful escape from Juba. Throughout the night, they spread rumors that the Northern soldiers in Juba had perpetrated a massacre of troops and civilians. These rumours had a terrible effect on the mutineers and on the civilians in Torit. Many of them decided to avenge the death of their brothers in Juba.[24]

It has to be recalled that Lieutenant Reynaldo was the mutineers' contact in Juba prior to the mutiny. The mutineers decided to give him command as of 20th August. Corporal Saturlino Oboya who was released from prison by his colleagues on 18th August, gave unconditional loyalty to Reynaldo owing to the major role he played in preparation for the mutiny by the later. Reynaldo was an active Lieutenant in Equatorial corps and indeed had the plot succeeded he would have got the post of Commander of the Equatorial Corps. He was the coordinator between the forces in Juba and the Torit garrisons on the one hand, and between the Equatorial Officer Corps and the Liberal Party on the other hand. Moreover, he seemed to have been trusted by all the parties involved more than any other officer in the Equatorial Corps. It was perhaps on that ground that he was handed the leadership of the mutiny.

In the afternoon of 19th August, the mutineers managed to establish contact with the British military authorities in Kenya.* They sent about four messages to the British forces there, urging them to send reinforcement in order to help in rescuing them from what they considered to be impending Northern invasion.

In one of these messages they said:

> The situation of Torit is still quite and our forces are still in their defensive positions. We are expecting dangerous disturbances this afternoon or evening or tomorrow. Please send a telegram about your arrival and the use of signal of British flag is very important for us to recognize you.[25]

A couple earlier, the rebels had sent three messages urging the British authorities in Kenya to send forces and informing them about the situation in Torit and in other Southern provinces, especially Juba. Of course the mutineers were not in a position to know what was taking place outside Torit. However, they were desperately in need of outside reinforcement and for this had to spin imaginary tales. It seems however, that up to August 19th, the British authorities in Nairobi were unaware of what was actually taking place in Torit and in Juba.

On 20th August, the British Colonial authorities in Nairobi, sent the mutineers the following message:

The Mutiny of the Equatorial Corps, August 1955

Reference to your messages to Likotong, (presumably a military garrison in Kenya), we have now learned from reports which reached us from Khartoum that you have mutinied. This is a very big crime and the British consider it a big mistake. Do not, I repeat, do not wait any British assistance. They are (the British) very sorry to hear what you have done and thus advise you to stop your rebellion. They advise you to inform all the other forces to stop the rebellion also. You must contact the Sudanese government by any possible means. The British are sure that a just and a comprehensive investigation will be carried out-please acknowledge the receipt of this message.[26]

Implementation of the original Plan

Convinced that outside reinforcement was not possible, the rebels decided to implement their original plan, which required them to confront an expected Northern counter action. According to this plan Lieutenant Reynaldo Loyola was to direct the operations using Torit as his headquarters. Lieutenant Madi Abu was to be in charge of surveillance and supplies. Lieutenant Albino Tombe would lead two platoons to Ngangala, twenty miles from Juba, where he would be joined by the arriving King's African Rifles from Nimule near the Ugandan border, sometime on the 20th of August.[27]

Lieutenant Albino did move the two platoons on the appointed date to Ngangala, but the king's African Rifles did not arrive as planned. It was also planned that Lieutenant Paul Ali Gbatala would cross to the west bank, near Juba, where he would try to regroup the escaping mutineers from Juba. In fact, he did cross to the West bank on 22nd August, but failed to attack Juba as envisaged.

Part of the plan was to send a platoon to Mongalla; the unit actually got to Mongalla but hurried back to Torit on 23rd August because of the shortage of food supplies. Moreover, the plan included a transfer of a platoon from Lueka (Loka) and another from Kapeota to be stationed at Torit. About two platoons were stationed at Torit airport in case Northern Forces tried to airlift any forces to the city.[28]

At about eleven o'clock, 20th August, two lorries carrying rebels arrived at Torit prison. They asked the police sergeant in charge of the prison to open the prison; the request was turned down three times. The two groups then opened fire; as a result 36 Northern merchants were wounded and five others were instantly killed; four women and eight children were also killed.[29]

It is important to point out that the spread and intensity of the mutiny in three Southern provinces varied depending on the degree of control exercised by Northern forces. In Juba and Malakal for example, the Northern forces were able to subdue the disturbance in a short time. Moreover, in those areas where Southern officials cooperated with the Northern administrators in the region, several Northern lives were spared; this was the case in Wau, Rumbek and Renk district.

In addition to those killed on 18th August and those who were shot in the Torit prison on 20th August, a Southern officer ordered on 25th August that the remaining Northerner Sudanese be

The Mutiny of the Equatorial Corps, August 1955

transferred to army cells in Torit military headquarters; all of these people were shot dead before they could reach their destination. On the same day two Northern merchants were also shot dead.[30]

In Kapeota a Northern officer, promised fair treatment as a prisoner of war, was murdered in his cold blood. A total of 35 Northern Sudanese were killed in Kapeota District alone.[31]

In Juba the news of the mutiny was received on August 18th at 10:30 a.m. Captain Salah Abdel Majid rushed to inform Lt. Colonel Al Taher Pasha Abdel Rahman Acting Commander of the Equatoria Corps about the news. Captain Salah then hurried to the Hagana platoon No-5 and ordered it to be ready for operations. Both Captain Salah and Lt. Colonel Al-Taher agreed that the two platoons of Southern corps, stationed two miles from Juba, were to be disarmed.[32] Captain Salah immediately asked the fifteen Southerners who were drivers of the Hagana platoon to hand over their arms and their cars. This request resulted in cross firing between Northern soldiers and the fifteen drivers. The Southern soldiers, who managed to escape before they were disarmed, and spread the news in the city that Southern troops were being killed by their Northern counterparts. Chaos and confusion ensued. It was during this confusion that Lieutenant Reynaldo Loyola managed to escape from Juba to Torit. Having disarmed all the Southern troops, police and prison warders' ammunition were also withdrawn by Northern officers. A curfew was decreed, and Juba airport was heavily guarded. Four Southerners were killed in Juba; no Northern deaths were reported.[33]

In Kejukeji news of the rebellion was received on 19th August at 2:00 p.m. The church leaders in Kejukeji managed to rescue the

Northern Sudanese in the district. A women and her child along with two Northern merchants escaped to Uganda safely.[34]

In Maridi the authorities received the news of the mutiny on 19th August. As a result of a limited mutiny of some Southern corps troops in the district, 13 Northerners were killed in Maridi; 3 in Amadi, 5 in Iba, 5 in Mundri and one Northerner near the village of Chief Jambo.[35]

In Yambio and Anzara the news of the rebellion reached the two districts on the same day of its occurrence. All the British officials employed by the Equatoria scheme at Anzara left the district to the Belgian Congo (now Zaire) using the company's cars. Along with them went the District Commissioner of Yambio. The total number of Northern Sudanese reported killed was 45. Elsewhere in Equatoria province in places such as Terekeka, Toli, Loka, Lenya and Rekon several Northern Sudanese officials and civilians were murdered. Southern soldiers, police and prison wardens who participated in these killing fled to the nearby bushes.[36]

In Malakal as early as 10th August, Major Mustafa al-Kamali, the Commander of the Southern Corps Platoon No. 4 at Malakal had planned precautionary actions aimed at disarming all the Southern troops in case of any disturbances. It has to be recalled that Platoon No.4 of the Southern Corps, stationed at Malakal, was ordered to leave for Khartoum on 19th August 1955. When the news of the Torit mutiny reached Malakal on 18th August at 11:30 a.m., Platoon No. 4 was asked to board the waiting boat. Instead of boarding, the troops chose to stay ashore. They requested the Commander to explain why their ammunition was not given

The Mutiny of the Equatorial Corps, August 1955

to them. The answer was that they were going to participate in a ceremony; hence they did not need ammunition. Throughout the day the authorities made certain that the news of the Torit mutiny should not reach the soldiers. At 10:30 p.m., following prolonged discussions, the corps' sergeant consented to the soldiers getting on to the boat. At 11:30 p.m., the boat finally sailed toward Khartoum.

Meanwhile, on 22nd August, a message was received from the Bahr El Ghazal Commissioner, Daud Abdel Latif, informing his Upper Nile counterpart that he was on his way to Malakal and that he and his senior officials had escaped from Wau. The news was received with some apprehension. The Upper Nile authorities concluded that the Torit mutiny had actually developed into a general uprising throughout the South. It was therefore decided to withdraw arms and ammunition from the Southern police. In the process, the arms depot guards, four in number, exchanged fire with the troops who had come to take over the arms depot. As a result of the cross fire in the police headquarters, 9 Southerners and one Northerner were killed, including a young Shilluk girl called Nyakat Nyato. Tension rose in the city, but no further disturbances occurred. In the other districts of the province, policemen, prison wardens and civilians ran away with whatever arms they could put their hands on. Desertions occurred in Khorfolous, Malut, Fanjak, Nasir, Akobo, Pibor, Bor, Bentiu, and in Gambella, a Sudanese administered district in Ethiopia. Compared to the manner in which the situation was handled in Equatoria and Bahr el Ghazal provinces the Upper Nile province authorities handled the situation cautiously and with the seriousness it deserved.[37]

REVOLUTION ON EQUATORIA MOUNTAINS

The news of the mutiny was received in Bahr El Ghazal capital on 18th August from the Ministry of Interior in Khartoum. It is worth mentioning that out of 286 officers and soldiers in Wau, the highest post held by a Southerner was that of Sergeant Akech. Soon after receiving the news, the Commanding Officer, Colonel Arwa Pasha, informed Sergeant Akech about the mutiny. The later informed his senior officer that, while he was able and willing to use his influence among the Dinka regulars in the army, it would be difficult for him to do the same among non-Dinka elements. The two men agreed that their cooperation was very essential if bloodshed were to be avoided in Wau. The next morning, survivors of the Yambio and Anzara disturbances arrived in Wau.

Among them was Lieutenant Nyang Nhial. On 20th August at 11:00 a.m. Satino Deng and Philmon Majok, members of Parliament, arrived in Wau from Khartoum. They met with Sergeant Akech and assured him that no Northern reinforcement would be flown to Wau. On the other hand, Lieutenant Nyang Nhial took over the command from Sergeant Akech on 22nd August, having learned that senior government officials had left the city. The decision to leave Wau was taken on 21st August by the leading Northern officials, including the Governor and the Commanding Officer, having been convinced that their presence would cause further disturbance in the province. Ironically, the departure of Northern Sudanese senior officials calmed down the situation in the city.[38]

In general, the report of the Commission of Inquiry did not include the number or the names of those who were wounded nor did it register names of some Southerners who lost their lives in

The Mutiny of the Equatorial Corps, August 1955

Equatoria. The commission report did, however, record that 12 Northerners were considered as missing. Some of those killed were difficult to identify; moreover many bodies were buried in groups. The list of recognized dead people throughout the South was as follows:[39]

Town	Northerners	Southerners
Torit	78	5 (drowned)
Kapeota	35	-
Kateri	9	6
Juba	-	4
Terekeka	7	-
Toli	6	-
Yei	32	1
Loka	17	-
Lenya	3	-
Maridi and surroundings	27	-
Yambio and Anzara	45	-
Malakal	1	9
Rumbek	1	1
	261	75

Total: 336

In addition to (6) people killed and two drowned in the Anzara disturbances of 26 July 1955.

The Sudan Government Reaction

Details about the mutiny reached Khartoum rather slowly. In fact, most of the news emanated from East Africa, where as pointed out earlier, the rebels had established contacts with the British authorities there.[40] The Governor-General Sir Alexander Helm Knox, who was on vacation in Scotland at the time, declared, on 19th August, a state of emergency throughout the three Southern provinces. The Council of ministers met also on 19th August and issued the following official statement:

> A mutiny broke out among two companies of the Equatoria Corps, Sudan Defense Force, in Torit town, Southern Sudan. Three Northern officers are missing, one of them believed killed. It is impossible to communicate with Torit. Details are therefore not yet available. Supplies and reinforcements are reaching Juba regularly and the situation is completely in the hands of the authorities who are closely watching all the Equatoria province. Bahr el-Ghazal and Upper Nile provinces are quiet and normal. We appeal to the nation not to listen to the biased rumors circulated by evildoers. The Government will take the necessary steps to maintain security and stability.[41]

In order to deal with the disturbances, the Sudanese government in Khartoum also asked the British government for air support to transport troops to the South. On August 20th the Commander of the Sudan Defense Force issued the following statement:

The Mutiny of the Equatorial Corps, August 1955

The reinforcement of the troops at Juba is still going on and everything is quiet in the town. The special force at Juba managed to recapture some military vehicles from the rebels. Contact with Torit is still impossible. The situation in other Southern provinces is quiet.[42]

In a statement to the press, the government spokesman accused the Egyptian government and blamed them for the mutiny. The spokesman, in particular, demanded an explanation of why an Egyptian diplomat was in Torit during the first week of August. The spokesman also blamed Southern MPs for their unwillingness to help in bringing the mutiny to an end.[43] Throughout the Sudanese government tried to give the impression that the mutiny was limited in scope, insisting that it was engineered by anti-government elements but fostered by Egypt. Ismail Ahmed al-Azhari's government, as a result, ordered the removal of all Egyptian officials from the three Southern provinces of the Sudan. The Egyptian officials working with the Irrigation Department in Malakal and Juba were put under surveillance.[44]

It was not until 22nd August that the government was able to contact the mutineers directly by wireless. On the above date the Prime Minister, Al Azhari, sent a message to the mutineers calling on them to surrender:

You have committed a big crime, but I want to make it clear to all of you, with my personal assurances and word of honor, that if you put down your arms now and you give in to the Sudanese government, a fair trial and comprehensive inquiry will be carried out on the causes of your mutiny. And each of you will be given full chance to explain his actions. If you are willing to do that, I will make arrangements for two or three Sudanese government agents to meet two or three of your representatives somewhere between Juba and Torit road. The agents of each group will move to the place of meeting holding white flags and when they meet, they will discuss the arrangements of your surrender. Please acknowledge the receipt of this letter now and after that send your full reply within 24 hours.[45]

On 23rd August, the rebels, having acknowledged the receipt of the Prime Minister's message, responded by pointing out that they would not give up their arms until all the army flown in from the North since 10th August were withdrawn. They further requested that British forces should take over the Northern Sudanese army defenses in the South and should supervise their surrender.[46]

The Prime Minister's response came on 24th August; in it he reaffirmed his previous promises. He gave the mutineers a further 24 hours. He went on to say:

It is illogical that you ask the Sudanese government to withdraw its Northern forces from Juba; they will not be withdrawn until everything calms down. The Sudan government must keep order and you went against law and order... You must fully understand the meaning of the word surrender. It means you put down your arms, and the

The Mutiny of the Equatorial Corps, August 1955

Northern forces will take you as prisoners (of war) and you will remain under arrest while a comprehensive and just inquiry is being carried out...I assure you that the Northern forces will not cross to the west bank. Do not listen to the rumors that they have already crossed. Please acknowledge the receipt of this message.[47]

For the second time the rebels rejected the Prime Minister plea. Instead, they called upon the Prime Minister to send United Nations representatives, along with Colonel Ismail Salim, the Equatoria Corps' Commander, to investigate the causes of the mutiny. They also demanded the withdrawal of Northern forces from Juba and their transfer back to Khartoum. The Prime Minister responded by insisting that he would not alter his offer and hence gave them a last warning to accept his terms within 24 hours. With this uncompromising message the contacts between the Prime Minister and the mutineers were terminated.[48]

The British Government Reaction

In response to the request of the Sudan government, the Governor-General of the Sudan, who was at the time in London, managed to win the approval of the British government to make Royal Air Force planes available for the transport of Northern Sudanese troops to the South.[49] The Foreign Office spokesman told the reporters on August 22nd that Britain would not send troops to the South, unless requested by the Sudanese government, and even then the British government had to study the request in all its aspects. He denied categorically any British involvement in the mutiny.[50] Meanwhile, before leaving for Khartoum, the Sudan Governor-General, Sir Alexander Knox Helm, told reporters in London on August 22nd that:

> It is important that the Sudanese government should restore immediately its authority in the South. Inquiry into the causes of the mutiny should be carried out. What is important is that there should be confidence between the Southern tribesmen and the government.[51]

On the other hand, the British Ambassador in Cairo, Humphrey Trevelyan, informed Major Salah Salim, the Egyptian Minister in charge of Sudanese Affairs, that Britain had rejected Egypt's proposals for a Sudanese round table conference and the dispatch of Egyptian and British troops to South Sudan to restore order after the mutiny.[52]

Upon his arrival in Khartoum from leave in Scotland, the Governor-General, Sir Alexander Knox Helm wired on the 25th August the following message to the Equatorial Corps in Torit:

> I am most deeply shocked by your mutiny. When I visited Torit last may, I was very pleased with the spirit and efficiency of the Southern Corps. I never thought that three months later you would bring shame and disgrace on the name of the Southern Corps by breaking the oath which each of you has taken to serve me truthfully and faithfully

The Mutiny of the Equatorial Corps, August 1955

and to obey lawful orders of your superior officers. As a supreme commander of the Sudan Defense Force I now ORDER YOU TO OBEY THIS DIRECT ORDER FROM ME and by facing like men the consequences of your acts you will help stop further bloodshed and to realize the disgrace of your mutiny. The Prime Minister of the Sudan has told you what surrender means... I myself now give you the same assurance. If you are ready to obey my order fully and without question I will send Mr. (William) Luce, who is my advisor and who was Deputy Governor of Equatoria in 1950 and 1951 as my personal representative to Torit to tell you the detailed arrangements for your surrender. You must acknowledge this message immediately and send me your reply within 24 hours.[53]

On the next day the Equatoria Corps in Torit responded to the Governor-General thanking him for his immediate return from England. They added that:

We will be very grateful if you could order the Northern forces in Juba to withdraw or at least to move a distance before we could surrender our arms. Or else we would kindly ask you to send British forces right away to safeguard the Southern troops during the surrender. Our fear came on 18 August 1955 when the drivers of the platoon No. 3 were asked by the troops in Juba to surrender their arms and were shot dead by the Hagana forces at Juba. We are telling the truth. We are not causing further bloodshed.[54]

The Governor-General rejected these demands outright and urged the rebels to accept his offer of 25th August; otherwise they would bear the consequences of their defiance.[55]

The British Government's position regarding the Torit mutiny and the Egyptian attempts to persuade London to mount a joint intervention was summed up by Lord Humphrey Trevelyan, the British Ambassador to Egypt at the time, who said:

> ...(S)alah Salim was right when he said that the Egyptians could not have created the mutiny, but they had certainly encouraged it. Egyptian propaganda and money had, for some time, been employed by the Egyptian Irrigation officials stationed in the Sudan under old arrangements to watch the level of the Nile. The Egyptians, presumably calculated that the Southerners could be brought to regard the Egyptians as their supporters against the North and that revolt in the South could bring about the fall of al-Azhari. Salah Salim appeared to know what was going on before the Governor-General was aware of it. He visited me late one evening in a state of great excitement to propose the dispatch of British and Egyptian troops to the South. It looked as if the plan was for the British troops to move out in due course and for the Egyptian troops to stay and restore the crumbling Egyptian position. We did not respond the Sudanese Government showed themselves surprisingly competent in dealing with the situation and Salah Salim's last effort failed.[56]

The Mutiny of the Equatorial Corps, August 1955

At the same time, suggestions of British intervention came also from the opposition parties: the Umma and the leftist groups, British government officials in Uganda (most of whom had previously served in Southern Sudan), former British Southern officials and from the mutineers themselves.57 Again, London responded with a firm rejection; possible air intervention was turned down as a precedent for any future Egyptian intervention in the South. The Southern Liberal Party for its part called for immediate action. In the final analysis it was apparent that both London and Khartoum had skilfully played down the importance of the mutiny in the public media. In a word, it was in their interest to belittle the August 1955 mutiny, if Egyptian intervention was to be avoided.[58]

The Egyptian Government Reaction

In Cairo, upon receiving the news of the mutiny, Major Salah Salim, the Egyptian officer in charge of Sudanese Affairs, made a point of capitalizing on the mutiny.[59] He rushed to the British Ambassador in Cairo, Sir Humphrey Trevelyan, and called on Britain for joint intervention in Southern Sudan. On Thursday August 25th, 1955, Major Salah Salim requested Prime Minister Gamal Abdel Nasser to convene a meeting of the Revolutionary Command Council to discuss the situation in the Sudan. In addition to the rest of the Revolutionary Command Council members, the meeting was attended by the Egyptian officials responsible for Sudanese affairs, including Khalil Ibrahim, Abdel al-Fatah Hasan and Husayn Dhul Faqar Sabri. They gave a report to the council on the situation in the Sudan, especially in the South.[60] They pointed out that news coming from the Sudan had revealed that Egyptian officials there had bribed several Southern and Northern Sudanese politicians; as a result it created anger among Egyptian allies in the Sudan who opposed bribery as a means of convincing them to unite with Egypt. This anger, they reported, had led several Sudanese who sincerely believed in Nile valley unity to refrain from cooperating with Egypt.[61]

In the same meeting, Major Salim described to the Council the gloomy situation in the Sudan. He pointed out that the mutiny in the South and the bloodshed that had followed was blamed on him by the Northern Sudanese. He told the Council that he feared retaliation against Egyptians in the Sudan. The solution to this dilemma, Salim argued, was for the Council to take a courageous decision supporting the independence of the Sudan up to then (Egypt was against independence of Sudan, unless it entailed unity with Egypt) so that it would appear as if Egypt, not Britain, was behind the independence of the Sudan. This move, Salim thought, would restore the confidence between Egypt and the Northern Sudanese.[62]

In the same meeting, Salah Salim gave his resignation to the Prime Minister, who accepted it, despite objections from Abdal-Latif Baghdadi, Kamal al-Din Husain and Hasan Ibrahim, who argued that:

> Salah Salim was carrying out the council's policy on the Sudan, and the policy was not his although he had committed some mistakes while implementing it.[63]

The Council finally approved Sudanese independence, and supported the struggle of the Sudanese to achieve it. 'Radio Cairo'

The Mutiny of the Equatorial Corps, August 1955

continued, however, to broadcast news of Northern troops "flown in by hired British aircraft attacking Southerners".[64] In a press conference, Major Salim strongly denied any knowledge of Egyptian involvement in the Mutiny, and accused the Sudanese government of fabrication against Egypt. He went on to say:

> The mutiny came as a result of a series of wrong actions by the Sudanese government. These actions included imprisonment of a Southern member of Parliament, Elie Kuze, which led to a clash between his supporters and the police at Nzara, in Yambio district; the disarming of the military units in the South and their withdrawal to the North. Egypt could not be accused of responsibility.[65]

In another press statement, Major Salim openly accused Great Britain of planning to separate Southern Sudan from the North. He went on to say that it was Great Britain's interest that the unity of the Nile valley-Egypt and Sudan-should not materialize.[66] Earlier Major Salim called for an all-Sudanese party emergency meeting to be held in Cairo in order to reassess the whole situation in the Sudan.

The British Foreign Office remained convinced that British interests required the immediate independence of the Sudan.[67] Hence, everything was done to speed it up. Similar contacts were made in Khartoum by the Egyptian diplomats, but the British administrators in the Sudanese capital maintained that the Southern corps had rebelled against an elected and legitimate government.[67] As a result, the Egyptian requests for joint intervention was regarded as counter productive.[68]

The End of the Mutiny

Repeating the Prime Minister's assurance that there would be a full inquiry into the causes of the mutiny, the Governor-General Sir Alexander Helm, sent on 26th August, what he called the last letter to the mutineers:

> I have received your letter with deep disappointment. You must fully understand that the Northern Forces cannot be moved from Juba nor will the British Forces be sent to the South. But I give you for the second time my personal assurance that if you surrender peacefully, the Northern Force will not, I repeat will not harm you. The Sudan Defense Force Commander himself will supervise your surrender and will make sure that his orders are promptly carried out by the Northern Forces. Mr. (William) Luce will also be there to supervise the surrender as my personal agent. And I must make it clear to you that, if you do not reply by 12:00 noon tomorrow 27th August, indicating that you will fully comply with my order without questions and accept to surrender, you must bear the consequences of what your refusal entails…This is my last letter to you. I pray to God that your answer will be acceptable.[69]

On 27th August Southern forces in Torit responded to the Governor-General by sending the following message:

> The forces in Torit have agreed to surrender. (I) will be very

The Mutiny of the Equatorial Corps, August 1955

grateful if you agree to give us 24 hours more so that we could call in the forces outside Torit. This is in order to avoid further bloodshed because they are not aware of your orders. Our positive response will reach you before twelve noon on 28th August. Trust that the Southern Forces will not, I repeat will not, dishonour your orders.[70]

The Governor-General agreed to give them 24 hours more to answer him. On 28th August, William Luce, the personal secretary of the Governor General, Mubarak Zarog, the Prime Minister's representative and the Commander of the Sudan Defense Force flew to Juba to arrange the surrender. At a meeting of representatives of the government and the rebels, somewhere between Juba and Torit, it was agreed that the mutineers would surrender themselves and their arms on 30th August.[71]

The Northern troops crossed to the Eastern bank and spent the night of August 30th around Torit as agreed upon. When they entered the city on the appointed date, they found 27 persons: two policemen, Lieutenant Oboya, the mutiny leader, his messenger, few army wardens, and some Northern Sudanese survivors who were in hiding with the Catholic mission among them was Dr. Anuar Khateb, an Egyptian medical Doctor.[72]

Several questions remain unanswered, as to why the Lieutenant Reynaldo chose to stay? Did he feel guilty? Why did his soldiers leave him behind? Did he believe Sir Alexander Helm's assurances? In the first place Reynaldo seemed to have been confused by the outcome of the rebellion. Being a junior officer in the army, he felt incapable of leaving a rebel group. Perhaps he convinced himself that all his backers notably the Liberal Party leadership, led him down. Throughout the mutiny none of those who supported him and his colleagues had shown any sort of sympathy, especially during the negotiations for their surrender. Another reason might be that he considered himself responsible for all that took place, especially the bloodshed that followed: after all he was the link between the soldiers and the politicians. Finally he seemed to no idea of what would happen had he left for the bushes of the South Sudan. In fact, apparently he seemed to have no plan to lead an armed movement in Southern Sudan.

Whatever the reasons were, the Cotran report concluded that the mutineers' were in general convinced that the Northern troops were going to kill them.[73]

Indeed, the rebels were right as later developments would show. Although the scattered rebels posed no significant military problem, the government tried to round them up and put them on trial. All 1,400 Southern troops in Equatoria province were considered mutineers. The Southern corps was officially disbanded. The mutiny was spontaneous as far as the participation of the non-Torit companies was concerned. Some of these companies were not informed about the mutiny, but responded spontaneously when it did take place; for example the garrisons in Yambio, Tambura, Rumbek, Nasir, Bentiu, and Bor reported without prior coordination with the Torit mutineers. The level of participation among the garrisons throughout the South was therefore determined by the extent to which they were free to act. But the momentum in favor of the mutiny seemed to have gained ground quiet quickly in the region. As for the participation of the local population, their reaction seems

The Mutiny of the Equatorial Corps, August 1955

to have been triggered by the rumours, which were circulated that Southern soldiers in Torit and Juba were murdered by their Northern colleagues. This might partially explain the random killing that followed the mutiny, especially in the Equatoria province. On the other hand it is very difficult to define what the mutineers really wanted, except that they were perhaps carrying out orders of some Liberal Party politicians.

On September 19th only 461 mutineers surrendered. Of the rest, 140 escaped into Uganda and about 780 were scattered all over the Equatoria province.[74]

By 15th December civil courts had issued 147 death sentences, of which the Governor-General, in his capacity as the head of state confirmed 121. The advocate of the rebels was Justice Ahmed Khair who appeared on their behalf. Almost half of the condemned were policemen the rest equally divided between soldiers and civilians.[75]

A proposal on public execution was turned down by Sir Knox Helm. Diplomatic efforts were made to negotiate the handing over of escaping mutineers to Uganda.[76] Some of these mutineers were eventually handed over to the Sudanese government.

Lieutenant Renaldo Loyola, the leader of the Torit mutiny, was executed in January 1956 following a closed-session of military trial; with his death, the government announced in February 1956 that the rebellion in the South had been crushed and law and order were restored.

End Notes

1. Rose El-Youssef (Cairo), 8 August 1955, p. 8; see also The Times (London), 29 August 1955, p. 6; also Time (New York), 29 August 1955, p. 17; Takrir Lajnat Tahkik al-Idari---, pp. 130-135.

2. *Time* (New York), 2 January 1956, p. 19; also see Takrir Lajnat Tahkik Al-Idari---, pp. 128-139.

3. On the North-South relations prior to the British departure from the Sudan see Dustan M. Wai, *African-Arab Conflict in the Sudan* (New York: Africana Publishing Company Co., 1981), pp. 64-68; also Oliver B. Albino, *The Sudan: A Southern Viewpoint*, (London: Oxford University Press, 1970), pp. 38-39; more details are given in Peter R. Woodward, "Is Sudan Governorable? Some Thoughts on The Experience of Liberal Democracy and MIlitary Rule" *British Studies for Middle Eastern Society Bulletin*, No. 2 (1987), pp. 137-149.

4. Martin W. Daly, *Imperial Sudan: The Anglo-Egyptian Condominiums, 1934-1956* (Cambridge: Cambridge University Press, 1991), pp. 385-88; John Howell explores the political background to the mutiny in "Politics in Southern Sudan," *African Affairs*, 72, No. 287 (April 1973), pp. 163-78. Also see *The Times* (London), 23 August 1955, p. 8.

5. Howell, *Politics in Southern Sudan*, pp. 163-78.

6. *An-Nahar* (Beirut), 20 August 1955, p. 1; Peter R. Woodward, "The South in Sudanese Politics, 1946-1956" *Middle Eastern Studies*, 6, No. 3 (October 1980), pp. 178-192. Most of the quotations given in this section are from the report of commission of inquiry. The text of the report used in this study is the Arabic translation. *The "Southern Liberal party" was founded in 1953 by several Southern Politicians prominent among them were Abdel Rahman Sule, Both Diu and Stanislaus Paysama.

7. Takrir Lajnat Al-Tahgig al-Idari..., p. 35.

8. Ibid., pp. 35-36.

9. Ibid., p. 34.

10. Ibid., p. 31-32.

11. Ibid., p. 32.

12. Ibid., pp. 32-33.

13. Ibid., p. 33.

14. *The Times* (London), 25 August, 1955, p. 8.

15. Albino. *The Sudan: A Southern Viewpoint*, pp. 36-39; Dustan M. Wai, "Political Trends in the Sudan and the Future of the South, " in *The Southern Sudan: The*

The Mutiny of the Equatorial Corps, August 1955

Problem of National Integration, edited by Dustan M. Wai (London: Frank Cass & Co., 1973), pp. 145-171.

16 George W. Shepherd Jr, "National Integration and the Southern Sudan," *The Journal of Modern African Studies*, 4, 2 (1966), pp. 193-212; also see Wai, *African-Arab Conflict in the Sudan*, pp. 64-67.

17 *An-Nahar* (Beirut), 20 August 1955; p. 1; also *Al-Hayat* (Beirut), 20 August 1955, p. 1; *The Times* (London), 20 August 1955, p. 6; Al-Ahram (Cairo), 20 August 1955, pp. 1 and 13.

18 Takrir Lajinat al-Tahgig---, p. 39.

19 Robert O. Collins, *Shadows in the Grass: Britain in the Southern Sudan, 1918-1956* (New Haven: Yale University press, 1983), pp. 457-58.

20 *Al-Musawwar* (Cairo), 26 August 1955, pp. 12 and 13; also Tahgrir Lajinat al-Tahgig----, p. 39.

21 Takrir Lajnat Tahkik al-Idari---, p. 40.

22 Ibid., pp. 40-41.

23 *Al-Ahram*, (Cairo), 22 August 1955, pp. 1 and 13.

24 Edgar O'Ballance. *The Secret War in the Sudan: 1955-1972* (Hamden, Connecticut: Archon Books, 1977), pp. 41-43; Praha Blanka Richova, "The Ethnic Conflict as the Factor of the State Coherency in Africa: The Case of the Sudan," *Archive Orientalni*, 59 (1991), pp. 289-312.

25 Takrir Lajnat Tahgig al-Idari---, pp. 40-41.

26 Ibid., p. 44.

27 *Al-Ahram* (Cairo), 2; August, 1955, pp. 1 and 11; also Takrir Lajnat al-Tahgig al-Idari---, pp. 53-54.

28 *Al-Ahram* (Cairo), 2, August 1955, pp. 1 and 11.

29 Takrir Lajnat Tahgig al-Idari----, pp. 49-50.

30 Ibid., pp. 41-42.

31 *An-Nahar* (Beirut), 12 August 1955, p. 1-4; al-Baghdadi, Mudhakkirat ---, pp. 280-302; Ramadan, A'Kzubat Istamar ---, pp. 173-175.

32 Takrir Lajnat Tahkik al-Idari----, p.

33 Eprile, *War and Peace in the Sudan*, pp. 42-48; an interesting illustration is given by Sam C. Sarkasian, "The Southern Sudan: A Reassessment," *African Studies Review*, 16 (1973), pp. 1-22.

34 See O'Ballance, *The Secret War in the Sudan*, p. 41; Eprile, *War and Peace in the Sudan*, pp. 43-45. What distinguishes the two writers, O'Ballance and Eprile from others is that they both conducted their research in Equatoria province. In fact,

they interviewed some prominent local leaders who had witnessed or participated in the mutiny.

35 Daly, *Imperial Sudan,* p. 386.
36 K.D.D. Henderson, *Sudan Republic* (London: Ernest Benn Limited, 1965), pp. 176-79; *Al-Hayat* (Beirut), 2 September 1955, p. 2.
37 Takrir Lajnat al-Tahkik al-Idari---, pp. 71-74.
38 Ibid., pp. 72-78.
39 Ibid., pp. 78-82.
40 Ibid., pp. 84-90.
41 The total figure of those killed before, during and after the mutiny is given in Tahkrir Lajnat al-Tahkik al-Idari fi Hawadith al-Junub, pp. 91-92; also see *Al-Hayat* (Beirut) 2 September 1955, p. 2; similar information are given by Eprile, *War and Peace in the Sudan,* p. 44.
42 *Al Hayat* (Beirut), August 23, 1955, pp. 1 and 7.
43 *The Times* (London) August 20, 1955, p. 6.
44 *Al-Ahram* (Cairo) August 21, 1955, pp. 1 and 11.
45 *The Times* (London) August 29, 1955, p. 8.
46 *Al Hayat* (Beirut), August 23, 1955, pp. 1 and 7.
47 See Wai, *African-Arab Conflict in the Sudan,* pp. 41-43; O'Ballance, *The Secret War in the Sudan,* pp. 41-44; For more details see Daly, *Imperial Sudan,* pp. 385-88; also *Al-Hayat* (Beirut), 24 August 1955, p. 2; *Al-Ahram* (Cairo), 21 August 1955, pp. 1 / 11.
48 *The Times* (London), 26 August 1955, p. 6.
49 Daly, *Imperial Sudan,* pp. 386-87; also see Cecil Eprile, *War and Peace in the Sudan, 1955-1972* (London: David and Charles 1974), pp. 40-44; Takrir Lajnat Tahgig al-Idari---, p. 44.
50 *Al-Ahram* (Cairo), 24 August 1955, pp. 1 / 5.
51 *The Times* (London), August 22, 1955, p. 6.
52 *Al-Hayat* (Beirut), August 23, 1955, pp. 1 and 7.
53 *Al-Ahram* (Cairo), August 23, 1955, pp. 1 and 13.
54 *The Times* (London), August 24, 1955, p. 6.
55 Takrir Lajnat Tahkik al-Idari----, pp. 46-47.
56 Takrir Lajnat Tahkik al-Idari ---, p. 47; *Al-Aharam,* (Cairo), 27 August 1955, pp. 1 - 13.
57 *Al-Ahram* (Cairo), 26 August 1955, p. 1 - 5.

The Mutiny of the Equatorial Corps, August 1955

58 Lord Humphrey Trevelyan, *The Middle East in Revolution* (London: MacMillan and Co., Ltd., 1970), pp. 17-18.

59 *The Times* (London), 22 August 1955, p. 6; also see *Al-Hayat* (Beirut), 22 August 1955, p. 2; *Al-Ahram* (Cairo), 7 August 1955, p. 7.

60 Both 'Radio Cairo' and the Egyptian press had capitalized the news of the mutiny. Major Salah Salim had at that time given several interviews to "Al-Ahram" newspaper. Daly, *Imperial Sudan*, pp. 386-88 and *Hansard Parliamentary Debates*, 17 November 1955, pp. 1467-1469.

61 *Time* (New York), 12 September 1955, p. 21; also *The Times* (London), 31 August 1955, p. 7; *Al-Musawwar* (Cairo), 26 August 1955, pp. 12-13.

62 Abdel A'zim Ramadan, *A'Kzubat Ista'mar al Masri Lil Sudan* (Cairo: al-Hey'at el-Masriyya al-A'mah Lil Ku'tab, 1988), pp. 173-175.

63 Abdul-Latif al-Baghdadi, *Mudhakhirat Abdul-Latif al-Baghdadi*. vol. 1 (Cairo: al-Maktab al-Masri al-Hadith, 1977), pp. 273-302.

64 Ibid., pp. 275-302.

65 Ibid., pp. 280-302.

66 Wai, *African-Arab Conflict in the Sudan*, pp. 64-68; also Woodward, "The South in the Sudanese Politics, 1946-1956", pp. 178-92; also refer to Daly, *Imperial Sudan*, pp. 382-88; *Rose El-Youssef*, (Cairo), 27 June, 1955, pp. 4-5/35; *Al-Ahram* (Cairo), 22 August 1955, pp. 1 - 13; *Al-Hayat* (Beirut), 30 August 1955, pp. 1 - 8.

67 *The Times* (London), August 22, 1955, p. 6; al-Baghdadi, Mudhakhirat ----, pp. 273-302.

68 *Al-Ahram* (Cairo), August 21, 1955, pp. 1 and 13; al-Baghdadi, Mudhakhirat ---, pp. 380-390.

69 *The Times* (London), 22 August 1955, p. 6; more details are given in *Al-Ahram* (Cairo), 23 August 1955; pp. 1/13; also *Al-Musawwar* (Cairo), 27 August 1955, p. 10; Ramadan, A'Kzubat Istamar al-Masri Lil Sudan, pp. 173-175.

70 *An-Nahar* (Beirut), 14 August 1955, pp. 1-4; al-Baghdadi, Mudhakkirat ---, pp. 273-302.

71 Takrir Lajnat al-Tahkik al-Idari---, p. 48; also Wai, *African-Arab Conflict in the Sudan*, p. 67; also see *The Times* (London), 27 August 1956, p. 6.

72 "Mutineers at Torit Agree to Surrender". *The Times* (London), 29 August 1955; p. 6; also *Al-Nahar* 30 August 1955; p. 1. More details are given in *Al-Ahram* 30 August 1955, p. 6; also Eprile, *War and Peace in the Sudan*, p. 45 and Daly, *Imperial Sudan*, pp. 285-88. The full text of the correspondence between the Governor-General and the Mutineers is given in the Takrir Lajnat al-Tahkik al-Idari---, pp. 48-94.

73 *Al-Hayat* (Beirut), 31 August 1955, p. 2; also *Al-Ahram* (Cairo), 30 August 1955, p. 6; also see "Vanished Rebells of Torit" *The Times* (London), 1st September 1955; p. 8.

74 *Al-Ahram* (Cairo), September 8, 1955, p. 6.

75 Details of the arrangements for the surrender of the Torit forces are discussed in *The Times* (London), 31 August 1955; p. 8; O'Ballance, *The Secret War in the Sudan*, pp. 42-43; also Eprile, *The War and Peace in the Sudan*, p. 45; also Wai, *African-Arab Conflict in the Sudan*, pp. 67-68; the comments of the Contran reports are found in: Takrir Lajnat al-Tahgig al-Idari---, p. 49; Reports on the surrender and the trials of the mutineers are found in *Al-Ahram* (Cairo), 9 September 1956, pp. 6/13; *Al-Hayat* (Beirut), 2 September 1955, p. 2; *The Times* (London), 31 August 1955, p. 8; See also *Al-Ahram* (Cairo), 11 September 1956, p. 6; also *Al-Ahram*, 16 September, 1955, p. 6. Most of the reports emanating from Cairo during September 1955 concentrated on the trials of the mutineers and the close down of all the schools in Southern Sudan. Eyewitness accounts were given and occupied large pages in the Egyptian press. The disband of the Southern corps was widely reported and commented upon by many Egyptian press commentators.

CHAPTER THREE

The Causes of the Torit Mutiny

The Commission of Inquiry

A few weeks after the Torit military rebellion Prime Minister Ismail Al-Azhari, appointed on September 8th, 1955, a commission of inquiry - officially known as Commission of Inquiry into the Disturbances in the Southern Sudan during August 1955. The Commission was chaired by Tawfiq S. Cotran, a Christian Palestinian judge and police magistrate a long time employee of the Sudan Condominium government. It included Khalifa Mahjoub, a Northern Sudanese General Manager in the Equatoria Scheme Board, as well as Chief Lolik Lado, a member of Parliament, from the Lokoya tribe, one of the Bari speaking tribes, located in Liria district in the region of Eastern Equatoria. The Commission, was instructed by the government to investigate the causes and not the consequences of the mutiny.[1] The Commission was to carry out investigation in Juba town or in any area or areas that the Chairman of the Commission deemed appropriate. The Commission work was restricted on administrative inquiry on the causes of the mutiny. Under no authority was it to investigate political or social aspects of the mutiny. The meetings and the hearings of the Commission were to be public or secret depended on the circumstances under which the Commission was working. The Commission was also authorized to appoint two advisors, preferably officers from the SDF, with the approval of the Defense Minister.[2] The Council of Ministers has charged the Commission with the following functions and/or powers:

To summon any person that can give information which may help the Commission in its investigation; the witness must be sworn in before giving his/her account of the events. The Commission was empowered to give orders and to send for books, papers and documents that it considered important and relevant to the inquiry.

The Commission may give orders, which must oblige a person summoned previously by the commission, but failed to appear before the Commission for unjustified reasons in the committee's opinion.

The Cotran Commission was empowered to pay any amount of money to any person that it summoned to one of its hearings, and who as a result of his appearance before the Commission, deserved financial compensation.[3]

After its formation, the Commission asked the Defense Minister to appoint two advisors on the military affairs; the advisors were Colonel Muhamed Pasha al-Tegani and Major Ali Husyan Sherfi.

The End of the Mutiny

The Commission began its assignment officially a week later, in Khartoum, then proceeded to the three Southern provinces and held several meetings and hearings in the places where the mutiny took place or in areas affected by the revolt. The Commission met 23 times in Khartoum, 16 at Juba, 3 at Malakal, 2 at Wau, 2 at Torit, 2 at Yei, 3 at Maridi, and one meeting each at Jumbo village and at Yambio. Moreover, the Commission visited Kapeota, Kateri, Gilo, Kagilo, Anzara, Loka, and Amadi district.[4]

During their presence in the South, the Commission noted that only a few Sudanese - Northerners and Southerners - voluntarily came forward to give their testimonies. The Commission did summoned a bigger number of people and was able to listen to the witnesses of the survivals, the tribal leaders, clerks, soldiers, politicians, missionary leaders, party leaders and members of parliament. In addition, the Commission obtained 24 government files related to the administrative aspects in the South. Despite its success in obtaining first-hand information on the mutiny, the Commission regretted what it considered to be unwillingness of the Attorney general council's refusal to meet the Commission members. Had they done so, "it could have helped the process and the progress of the inquiry smoothly." The Commission submitted its report to the Minister of Interior on February 18th, 1956. The report was published both in Arabic and in English.[5]

It is worth pointing out that most of the observers would, perhaps, underestimate the effects and the importance of some or almost all the reasons outlined by the Cotran Commission to be behind the outbreak of the Torit Mutiny. Almost all the Southern politicians prior to and on the eve of the mutiny had tended to react to the events, more than actually participating in making them. The South was an immature political community; and representative politics meant very little to its average population. Even the politicians themselves were much identified with the family and ethnic affiliation and more importantly by the extent to which they seemed to be against or for the central government policies in the South.6

By and large, on the eve of the independence and while the Southern politicians were engaged in political bargaining in Khartoum with Northern counterparts as well as Egyptians and British, the average Southern Sudanese was engaged in circulating rumours about British departure and the fears of its aftermath. Added to this, it seemed that Southern population had all along taken for granted whatever the politicians told them about North-South relations, real or imaginary. Therefore, the reasons described by the Cotran Report and the ones outlined below, would seem insignificant in the eyes of a sophisticated and a mature politically socialized society, which the Southern Sudan was not one at the time.[7]

The British Factor

It is within the context of the circumstances mentioned above, regarding the significance of the causes of the mutiny, that one may appreciate the importance of the findings of the Commission of Inquiry. In its report, the Commission of Inquiry had blamed and considered the British Southern policy to be one of the major reasons that had widened the political gap between the South

The End of the Mutiny

and the North. Between 1920 and the 1930 for instance, several Ordinances and Regulations were issued to form what become known as British Southern policy, all of which aimed then to:

…build up a series of self-contained racial or tribal units based upon indigenous customs, traditional usage and beliefs.[8]

British administrators in the South were empowered to prohibit Arabs from the Northern provinces from entering the three Southern provinces whether to trade, hunt or for any other objective, unless they had obtained a special permit. Indigenous Southern languages were encouraged; English was proclaimed the *lingua franca* in the South and Sunday became the day of rest instead of Friday. Arabic names, customs and dress were officially banned. In the three Southern provinces Northern Sudanese traders were encouraged to leave the region, the reluctant ones being forced to do so. These measures were intended to restrict Egyptians, Northern Sudanese and other West African Muslims to undertake activities, which in accordance with Colonial view would influence and negate the administration policy followed in the South.

By 1940, these Ordinances and Regulations had had far reaching effects on the economic development of the South. On the educational plane, Christian missionaries were entrusted with the task of educating Southerners. In other words, the 1930 Southern Policy succeeded in closing off the South; thus, the Southern region began to develop as a separate entity both in political and economic terms.[9]

In December 1946 for example, the Civil Secretary, Sir James Robertson, reversed the 'Closed Districts Policy' of 1930 and decided that the future of the Southern provinces should be a fusion with the North. The new policy came into operation at time when the two parts of the country had developed into distinctive political entities. The new Southern policy was based upon the fact that:

> Geography and economics, combine.... to render them (Southerners) inextricably bound for future development to the Middle-Eastern and Arabicised Northern Sudan: and therefore, to ensure that they shall, by educational and economic development, be equipped to stand up for themselves in the future as socially and economically the equals of their partners of the Northern Sudan in the Sudan of the future.[10]

The British Southern policy until 1946 therefore, had been instrumental in hindering the free association of the Sudanese among themselves. There was not enough time for the two parties-Southerners and Northerners-to learn about each other when the 1930 British Southern policy was abandoned. The 'Closed Districts' policy had also created unbalanced economic development in the two regions. Thus, when independence approached, the Southern Sudanese had developed some sort of fear that they would soon be handed over to the more advanced Northerners. Added to this the fact that the British educational and economic policies in the South had created Southern bitterness against the North, it became obvious on the eve of the independence that the north would become the heir of the political power in the country. The British Southern policy was therefore, considered by the Northerners to be a contributing factor to backwardness of the South. To the Southerners however, both the British and Northern Sudanese were responsible for political, economic and social underdevelopment of the South.[11]

As mentioned earlier, the Cotran Commission was restricted to concentrate its investigation on administrative aspects of the mutiny; thus, it did not report on any political role played by the Egyptian or the British governments. However, the Egyptian involvement in the mutiny in particular was very important and deserves a special attention.

The Egyptian Connection

Traditionally, the National Unionist Party, NUP, since its formation in 1949, favoured some form of the Sudan's unity with Egypt. On the eve of independence, NUP's position on unity with Egypt gradually changed, leading eventually to an open antagonism between the NUP and the Egyptian government in 1954. Faced with this new reality, the Egyptian Minister in charge of Sudanese affairs, Major Salah Salim, began to contact Southern Sudanese members of NUP. These links became known as early as June 1955 with some Southern Liberal Party members, covertly transforming this new alliance into an idea of creating political relations between Southern Sudan and Egypt. Employees of Egyptian Irrigation Department, stationed at

Malakal and Juba, started to distribute anti-Northern pamphlets, while 'Radio Cairo' broadcast in Southern languages and criticized Al-Azhari's Southern policies.[12]

The Egyptian-Southern new relationship was necessitated by two main developments: NUP-Egyptian relations had witnessed, as early as April 1954, a severe breakdown. Al-Azhari had tried to play down his party's rejection of unity with Egypt, but he had to announce openly his call for an independent Sudan in August. Secondly, having lost a long time ally the Egyptian government needed another Sudanese ally, through whom it could manoeuvre against the British government during the Anglo-Egyptian negotiations over the Suez Canal Zone. Thus, those Southern Sudanese politicians who had shown willingness to do business with Major Salim were received well in Cairo.[13]

It has to be recalled that leading members of the Liberal Party were in touch with some officers in Torit, the seat of the Equatoria Corps mutiny. During the months of June and July 1955, it was also reported that some leaders* of the would-be mutiny had received prolonged visits from two Egyptian officials accompanied by prominent pro-Egyptian Southerners.[14]

There seemed to have been an Egyptian plan or scenario aimed at a mutiny in the South. The Scenario went like this:

The troops of the Equatoria Corps who were scheduled to travel to participate in the ceremonies of the evacuation from the Sudan of British and Egyptian troops should be told that they would be killed while in Khartoum. If the Torit Corps out of fear had rebelled, the scenario goes on, other

The End of the Mutiny

Southern garrisons at Juba, Yambio, Yei, Malakal and Wau, with whom the plotters at Torit had established contact, would follow suit. Once the plot was carried out as envisaged, Cairo would demand that instead of pulling out, the British and Egyptian governments should airlift troops to the South in order to rescue the people of the region from what its press called "their Northern oppressors.[15]

In this way, Anglo-Egyptian evacuation would have been halted and new arrangements, would have to be made. Major Salim's move could be considered as an attempt to use the South as an instrument to strengthen Egyptian influence in the Sudanese politics. Ironically, the South had often been a pawn used by London against Cairo and Khartoum. Thus, the South became a last desperate action to redirect the Egyptian political objectives in the Sudan. Again, the question that arises is: would it follow from the above scenario that the Torit mutiny was not entirely spontaneous and that the Egyptians were involved? The fact that none of the alleged Southern instigators were tried seemed to confirm the above scenario. In fact the Egyptian press* on the eve of the mutiny had conducted several interviews with some prominent Southern politicians. In all of these interviews they had hinted to the possibility of a mutiny as a last resort against Al-Azhari's refusal to implement a Federal System in the country.

Moreover, when the Cotran Commission completed and submitted its report in February 1956, one month after Sudanese independence, it omitted any reference to Egyptian or British involvement in the mutiny. The "Deal", if one may term it so, seemed to have developed along the following lines: as mentioned above, surprisingly, Egypt consented to unconditional independence of the Sudan; Great Britain on the other hand, signed an understanding agreement with Egypt allowing its troops to remain in the Canal zone for a few more years. Prime Minister Al-Azhari for his part got away with what the Egyptian press described as his betrayal. Those Southern Sudanese who engineered the Torit rebellion, and who during the first weeks of August 1955 frequented Cairo, went freed and unpunished.

The victim, perhaps, was Major Salah Salim who lost his job. He was blamed for the deterioration of relations between Khartoum and Cairo on the one hand, and between Cairo and London on the other. He resigned on 25 August from both the Revolutionary Command Council and from the Sudanese Affairs, a move gladly welcomed with relief by both Khartoum and London.[16]

Judging from its press coverage of the August events; it seemed that Cairo had played some part in the revolt. However, like the British and Al-Azhari, Major Salim had tried to play politics; but again, the Egyptian involvement in the mutiny was not the only cause, but just one of many factors, which culminated into that bloody rebellion.

The Communist Element

The Communist Element in the Mutiny was another cause reported by the Commission of Inquiry. The Sudan Communist Party, first called the Sudan Movement for National Liberation, was formally

The End of the Mutiny

created in 1946, as an offshoot of the Egyptian Communist Party. The party later on developed an Orthodox, Moscow oriented wing led by Abdel Khaliq Mahjoub. In 1957 for the first time it contested elections through the anti-Imperial Front.* The Tommunist Party's penetration among the workers in the Zandeland and Moruland in Western Equatoria, started as early as December 1954. This communist infiltration was carried out by Northern and some Egyptian officials working in the Equatoria Industrial Projects, the Anzara Cotton Mill. In this Cotton Mill, active Union Workers had translated several pamphlets, which were written by Anti-Imperial Front members. These pamphlets were distributed among the local tribal leaders, government officials and even the local population.[17]

Some leaflets went as far as attacking the government policy of unequal pay for the Northern and Southern workers. At one point, some pamphlets called for a 'Southern local government' within a united Sudan. It was reported that in January and February 1955, prominent Anti-Imperial Front officials visited Nzara and other parts of Equatoria, and while there recruited many Southerners. One of the well-known activists was a certain Benjamin Basara, assisted by an Egyptian medical officer in Maridi district.[18]

Normally published in English, the tone of the leaflets varied depending on the audience to which each was addressed. Some emphasized the effectiveness of collective industrial strikes in claiming wage increases; others described the causes of what they considered to be Southern poverty and the means to fight them. Yet, others criticized the Northern Sudanese administration for not raising the wages of workers in the South. In one of these pamphlets the anti-imperialists complained that:

> Our economic standard must be raised by the Government. And this by seeing that things are sold in the shops at reasonable prices, and also that our local cash crops and other articles are bought from us at fair prices. It is too much to buy our local cotton at 1 1/2 piaster per bottle and after weaving its dumuria (cloth) at Nzara, it is sold to us for 13 piasters per yard. That is simply cheating because we are yet largely ignorant and backward."[19]

Some leaflets went as far as advocating 'local autonomy' for the South. In one of the pamphlets, signed by 'Southern Anti-Imperial Front' the Front demanded in December 1954 that:

> Malakal, Wau, Juba should be states, each having its own parliament; but the central Southern parliament should be at Juba and from this Juba central Southern parliament members should be selected to represent us in Khartoum Central Sudan parliament. In this way, we shall have our own Governors, District Commissioners, etc., but as far as we are going to be ruled by Northerners as it has began now, there is no difference for us with the time when the English were our rulers, and worse still it means very surely that were are to be only slaves.[20]

The logical question that follows is: were the communist activities in Equatoria province instrumental in the outbreak of the August 1955 mutiny? Despite their political activity and mobilization in Equatoria and among worker unions and intellectuals, there was no evidence, which suggested that the communists were influential enough to aggravate a general revolt in the South, which led to the Torit mutiny. After all, the propagators of communist orientation in the South were Northerners. On the contrary, evidences suggest that the peoples of the South did not at that stage understand or care about Marxism or Leninism. Even the Southern intellectuals of the 1950's seemed not to care about abstract communist theories, although communist slogans such as 'equal pay for equal work and three parliaments in Juba, Wau, and Malakal', interested them.[21] In other words, none of the veteran Southern Liberal Party members became a member of the Sudan communist party.

Therefore, it is fair to conclude that the influence of the communist propaganda among Southern elite did not overstep the workers' desire to raise their wages using communist slogans.

The prevailing economic hardship, in addition to the existing political tensions were perhaps more pressing then the communist instigation against the government to cause the disturbances of August 1955. But perhaps the importance of the communist element in the mutiny lies in that communist ideas were propagated in Equatoria where the mutiny took place. In fact some of the future guerrilla officers in Western Equatoria were worker union leaders of the Nzara Cotton Mill.

The Sudanization Factor

The 'Sudanization' of the Government institutions was yet another important reason given by the Cotran Commission, and has considered it to be behind the Torit mutiny. In accordance with the Anglo-Egyptian Accord of February 12th, 1953, which had officially consented to self-determination of the Sudan, the duties of the 'Sudanization' committee were to complete the Sudanization of the administration, the police, the Sudan Defense Force or any other Government body. The Committee was scheduled to complete its assignment within a period not exceeding three years. In addition to its consultative role, the Committee was empowered to recommend to the Council of Ministers principles to be adhered to in the Sudanization process.[22]

Seniority, experience and expediency were to be the criteria for elevation, recruitment and retirement of the government civil servants. Appointed by the Prime Minister on 20th February 1954, the Committee immediately began its work and by June 20th 1954, it disclosed that there were 1,111 British civil servants and 108 Egyptian officials in the Sudan government. Among them, about two thousand civil servants opted for voluntary retirement from the service, having been guaranteed huge gratuities.[23]

Prior to the mandate of the Sudanization Committee, the National Unionist Party, NUP, which won the majority votes in the first Sudanese National elections in November-December 1953, had promised regional autonomous institutions for the South. In its election campaign, the NUP policy in the South was outlined as follows:

> Our approach to the question of Sudanization shall always be first and domestic, not only shall priority be always given to Southerners in the South, but also the employment of

The End of the Mutiny

the Southerners shall be greatly fostered in the North, especially in the highest ranks of the Central government service. Not only government jobs but also membership in different local government institutions, development committees, etc., shall be as far as possible in hands of competent Southerners in the Southern provinces.[24]

Similar promises were made by the Umma Party, the Sudanese Communist Party and the other Northern political parties.

The process and the progress of the Sudanization in the South were rapid and trickier than in the North. In fact, in some districts in the South, the physical presence of a British District Commissioner personified the government existence and therefore his departure from the district without replacement meant the end of the government in that area. In Bahr el-Ghazal province for example, the British posts were first Sudanized in June 1954, and in September all the remaining British civil servants were notified to leave their districts. In like manner, a similar schedule was followed in the Upper Nile and Equatoria provinces.[25]

At the same level of rapidity, the order to start the Sudanization process of the Equatoria corps was received by the Commanding officer in June 1954. Within five weeks, the Sudanization of the corps was completed. On 29th July 1954, all the British personnel including the Commanding Officer, Lt. Colonel W.B. Brown, sailed by steamer from Juba to Khartoum. Commenting twenty-seven years later on the urgency of the process, Lt. Col. Brown had this to say:

When I told sol Talim (training Sergeant Major) about

our impending departure, he first refused to believe it. Eventually, having accepted the news, he said 'there will be war down here'...Although we were not *au fait* [sic] with all the political bargaining which had been going on in Khartoum, Cairo and London, we felt that after (50) years of successful administration in the Sudan, a most appalling mistake was now being made of the handover of the South; and that our troops – and, in fact, all the people in the South were being badly let down.[26]

If Lt. Col. Brown was disappointed, the Southern politicians, who watched with anger and alarm, as Northerners smoothly succeeded the British across the region, were not only disappointed, however, indeed looked at the process as the changing of one master for another. The decision to elevate only (6) Southerners out of the (800) remaining not sudanized civil service posts, was considered by the outgoing British officials as the single worse act of 'absurdity' in the history of the Southern Sudan during the colonial era.[27]

Reactions to the results of the Sudanization Committee varied depending on where each Sudanese political group or individuals stood. While admitting their educational limitations, Southern intellectuals nevertheless, blamed the Northern dominated governments for the unbalanced results:

"The results of Sudanization confirmed the feeling in the South that the region was being cheated and that it lot in the future was to be dominated and exploited by the North."[28]

Similar remarks went as far as accusing the North of trickery and hypocrisy:

The End of the Mutiny

When Sudanization was completed, only four junior posts of Assistant District Commissioner and two *mamurs* were given to the South. There was no excuse for this because a pro-Egyptian clerk at Juba provincial headquarter (a Southerner) was promoted and transferred to the North as a deputy governor.[29]

At the other extreme, Northern politicians were obstinate in emphasizing that the British Colonial power was solely responsible for the results of the Sudanization commission:

The list could not simply include any Southerner since none of them was qualified and experienced enough for those posts. The blame for that however, does not rest with Northerners, it rests with those responsible for training and educating the Southerners, the missionaries and the British administration.[30]

Nonetheless, some Northern Sudanese did acknowledge the Southern suspicions, nurtured over fifty years, but turned into hostility by the results of the Sudanization:

...(A)s the posts held by Southerners at the time, were by far fewer and more junior to those held by Northerners, and as they lacked seniority, experience and qualifications, Southerners were not much affected by the Sudanization. This was not only disappointing to the educated Southerners, but it was also looked upon as the changing of one master for another...The Sudanization

Committee in the best traditions of British Civil Service, allocated the posts based on its principles, hence it was not the Northerners to be blamed, but the British who taught and ruled Souterners.[31]

Disregarding these contradictory views of Southerners and Northerners the fact remains that what Southerners finally got was much less than what they were promised or, at least, made to believe that they would get. The inevitable outcome was that the Southern politicians and government employees were alienated and even the average citizen and eminently the illiterate were becoming hostile to the government authority and to the presence of the Northern administration. When in October 1954 the ruling NUP politicians, including Al Azhari, toured the South, in an attempt to ease the tension, the delegation was booed and ill-received everywhere it went throughout the region.[32]

The Prime Minister announced a rise in the salaries of the police, prison warders and clerks to be equal with Northern clerks, with immediate effect. This gesture, the first ever to be taken by the government, was considered by Southerners as a bribe. Added to this unwelcome gesture, the Prime Minister came into an open conflict with the only two Southern ministers in the cabinet, Bullen Alier and Dak Deth, over the results of Sudanization. One of them resigned and the other was sacked.

Commenting on the general situation at the time, one of the outgoing southern ministers was quoted as saying it has become a routine that:

> Each boat and aircraft brought Northerners for appointment to the administration, police or the army in the South; the

flow at times looked like an invasion.³³

By this time some Southern politicians had begun an open campaign threatening the use of violence, or at least to oppose the pending withdrawal of the British and Egyptian troops from the Sudan, if their political grievances were not considered. Slogans such as 'out with the Arabs' and 'civil war' were beginning to circulate in the South.³⁴

Al-Azhari government's Attitude

In August 1954, the government issued a warning in which it stated that it was aware of the 'conspirancies' that were being worked out in the South. It threatened the use of an iron fist in dealing with any Southerner who dared or attempted to destroy national unity, a direct reference to the Southern Liberal Party, which was holding a conference at the time in Juba. In response to these threats, the slogan 'Our Northern friends will use force against us' was then coined and circulated by Southerners.³⁵

It seemed that the Southern elite had assumed that as they provided the small political representation the South had, so too they would provide its officials. Thus, their exclusion from the government posts had, first, turned them against the Northern administrators serving in the South, hence affecting the transfer of power in the region. Secondly, it turned Southern politicians, now grouped into the Southern Liberal Party, against the government, which had endorsed the results of Sudanization. It was the

Prime Minister's opinion that the government should and must use all its strength to implement the Anglo-Egyptian Agreement of February 1953 both in letter and in spirit. It was al-Azhari's belief that the government should not be lenient in implementing the above agreement, since it had the army and police at its disposal.

By and large, Al-Azhari was convinced that the British, in spite of their apparent cooperation, had finally given up all hope of maintaining some form of influence in the Sudan and especially in the Southern Sudan. Therefore, any outbreak of disturbances in the South would give them the opportunity for intervention, which might delay Sudan's progress to independence.[36]

In the final analysis, the report of the Sudanization Committee seemed to have confirmed into the minds of the Southern Sudanese every suspicion, real or imaginary, about the intentions of the Northern dominated government. They looked at the transition as if they would indeed be treated as second class citizens.[37] The Commission of Inquiry seemed to have reached the same conclusion when it stressed that:

> We feel that Southerners had genuine grievance because they found themselves holding junior posts in their national government."[38]

The Liberal Party leadership also seemed to have concluded that military rebellion was more effective than political bargaining, hence the Torit Mutiny. On the other hand, in his rush to consolidate his political strength, al-Azhari probably moved too quickly in his efforts to Sudanize the British administration in the South.

The End of the Mutiny

By imposing Northern Sudanese in the South, he set the theatre for an internal crisis, which later had proven more difficult than the question of unity with Egypt.

Early in July 1955, a false telegram, purportedly having been signed by the Prime Minister, Ismail Al-Azhari, was circulated in the Southern provinces. The alleged telegram, printed on official paper, was addressed to the Northern administrators serving in the South:

To all my administrators in the three Southern provinces: I have just signed a document for self-determination. Do not listen to the childish complaints of the Southerners. Persecute them, oppress them, ill treat them according to my orders. Any administrator who fails to comply with my order will be liable to prosecution. In three months time all of you will come around and enjoy the work you have done.[39]

It is difficult to proof the authenticity of the alleged telegram and the Cotran Commission did not hesitate to declare it 'false and forged.'[40] Moreover, it was unlikely that the Prime Minister could have sent such a message to his administrators. Nevertheless, the importance of the message rested on its existence, and the attention paid to it throughout the South. On the other hand, the content, and to some extent the essence of the alleged telegram, seemed to reflect the attitude of some Northern administrators serving in the region.[41]

Also in July 1955, it was reported that the District Commissioner (DC) of Yambio and his assistant, forced the tribal chiefs of the district to affix their signatures to a statement, written on their behalf, supporting the government policy in the South. This telegram, sent in the name of thirteen chiefs, had many repercussions.[42]

The dispatch of the telegram coincided with the presence of a Southern Liberal Party member of parliament, Elia Kuze, who was at the time holding political rallies and meeting with his constituents. When he learned about the telegram, allegedly sent by the chiefs of his area, he grasped the opportunity and organized more public meetings in which he demanded the removal of chiefs who were supposed to have signed the message. In one of these rallies, a strong-worded resolution denounced the action of the chiefs and demanded for their deposition. In addition, the attendants denounced the DC's interference in politics.

Informed about Kuze's reaction, the chiefs lodged a complaint to the District Commissioner against Kuze and his supporters. The DC concurred with their complaint and signed a court summones.[43] Mr. Kuze, who was attending a Liberal Party conference in Juba, was detained by the police and sent back to Yambio for trial. Elia Kuze, along with Metre Mabo, Basonia Jambo, Singano Gabduro, Timothy Buati and Basia Yuku, were brought before the court on July 25th, 1955. Their charge was based on section 441 of the Sudan Penal Code. Their accusation was 'criminal intimidation'. In fact, they were sentenced by the chiefs' court consisting, in part, of those chiefs whose deposition they had demanded. The chiefs argued that the accused had on July 7th, 1955, at a political rally, resolved that the chiefs who signed the declaration of support for the government be removed from their offices. The chiefs found the accused guilty and sentenced each to 20 years imprisonment.

The DC, who was present in the courtroom, explained to the

The End of the Mutiny

chiefs that two years was the maximum sentence laid down by the law for such an offense. The sentences were thus reduced to two years each. While the court was in progress, and soon after the sentence was passed, a crowd of about 700 people spontaneously gathered outside the courtroom. The DC called in troops who having failed to persuade the crowd to disperse peacefully resorted to using tear gas. Amidst the confusion, two Northern Sudanese merchants* shot at the crowd, killing eight and injuring eleven people.[44]

The trial was referred to by the Cotran Commission as a 'farce and usurpation of the machinery of justice." Moreover, the trial had caused a great disappointment among Southern politicians and members of parliament because the District Commissioner's motive for the trial was simply the restoration of his own prestige and that of the thirteen chiefs.

Secondly, some members of the court were themselves involved in sending the declaration; hence they were in fact sitting as judges in their own case.

Thirdly, the trial was contrary to the spirit and intention of the chiefs' court's ordinance, which legislated for the trial of ordinary offences, and was not to be used for the trial of political offenders.

Fourthly, it was in the opinion of Southern Mps unlawful to try a member of parliament by chiefs' court since government officials included the Mps, were exempt from its jurisdiction.

Finally, no consideration was taken by the court of section 7(3) of the chiefs' court's ordinance which provided that attention be paid to the age and character of the first offenders.[45] The report of Commission of Inquiry emphasized that:

REVOLUTION ON EQUATORIA MOUNTAINS

"The fact that the DC himself interfered in politics in such a way is deplorable both in a moral and in an administrative sense...A population, which was passively anti-Northern was transformed, by such administrative meddling, into becoming actively so. The telegram of support for that matter, would not create such excitement, if it had been the spontaneous feeling of the people."[46]

One day after Elia Kuze's trial, 26th July 1955, disturbances broke out at Nzara, 16 miles from Yambio District, the industrial centre of Zande scheme. The violence occurred when sixty Southern workers threatened to strike if they were not given more pay. Early in July, the management of the Equatoria Project Board had dismissed some 300 Southern workers. The dismissals were accompanied by the appointment of extra Northern staff. When the Board turned down the workers' request, a crowd of 250 workers from the weaving and spinning mills staged a demonstration. The strikers were later joined by unemployed and other civilians in town. Armed with spears, bows and arrows, eventually swelling the crowd to a thousand. The strike got out of hand and looting began. Reinforcement consisting of five policemen, each with a tear gas bomb, and eleven Equatoria corps soldiers arrived from Yambio. Being too small in number to quell the demonstration, the soldiers panicked opened fire, killing four and fatally wounding two.[47] The Assistant District Commissioner, Mohamud Husein and Lieutenant Mu'tasim Abdel Rahman were blamed for their inability to control the situation and that they:

Were young in age and inexperienced and may be they were frightened when they saw the huge crowd. Thus, they had to resort to unlawful tactics. In any case, whether the incident was carefully handled or not, the effect of the incident itself in the Southern minds was bad for they considered it as the beginning of the war (The August 1955 rebellion).[48]

The effect on the morale of the Equatorial corps troops, having to fire on their fellow Southerners, appeared to have been considerable. According to Cotran Commission Report, instead of investigating the cause of Nzara demonstration, a further threatening ultimatum from Khartoum was circulated and broadcast on 'Radio Omdurman'.[49]

Psychological Factors

In addition to the direct causes discussed above, the Commission of Inquiry listed what it considered as minor or indirect grievances, which it has classified as psychological, which also had far reaching effects on South-North relations.

First, some Northern Sudanese, including high officials in the administration, referred to the Southern elite as half-educated. This attitude was condemned by the Cotran Commission:

Education is a relative term and largely a matter of opinion, but experience has taught time and again even nations with long history of colonial rule that it always pays to gain the confidence of the intelligensia whether they are fully educated, half- educated or quarter-educated."[50]

The conduct of calling Southerners half-educated had developed some sort of inferiority complex among Southern educated class vis-a-vis their Northern counterpart; hence, augmented the cleavage between the South and North.

Secondly, some Northern merchants or Gallaba* had often referred to Southerners as a 'abid (slaves); this attitude, which was widespread in the three Southern provinces, had had great psychological effect on Southerners; and reminded them of the Northern Sudanese historical role in the slave trade in the nineteenth century.[51]

Thirdly, in addition to the Northern merchants' contempt of nakedness, Northern Sudanese traders and some government officials were unwilling to mix with Southerners. In fact, throughout the South, Northerners had their own social clubs separate from those frequented by Southerners.[52]

The Cotran Commission report came to be regarded as one of the most important documents on the Torit mutiny. The impartiality of the proceedings and findings of this report has not been seriously questioned by either Southerners or Northerners and its objectivity and balanced assessment was widely recognized and praised by both sides.

However, while recognizing the impartiality of the report, Northerners and Southerners viewed it political significance differently. A Northerner may quote the report as a proof of Southern

The End of the Mutiny

error in opting for the use of force as the only means of solving national political differences. A Southerner on the other hand, would cite the report as proof of the many blunders committed by Northern administrators serving in the South.*

Taking position on the impartiality of the report, some Southern politicians have repeatedly pointed out that Cotran Commission was set up by Prime Minister Al-Azhari, but its findings were submitted to and made public by another Prime Minister from an opposing political party. However, regardless of the way in which politicians used or abused the Commission's report, the fact remains that the central authority in Khartoum succeeded in creating an impartial Commission of Inquiry and allowed it to freely publish its findings.[53]

In view of what has been discussed, the mutiny could be summed up into and considered as a direct reaction against the decision of the British government in December 1946 that the future policy regarding the three Southern provinces should be a union with the North. The British at the same time knew that the country, the people, the religions and in particular the spread of development of the two regions, which they were solely responsible for, were completely different.

Secondly, the abandonment of the safeguards for the South by the British government when the Anglo-Egyptian Agreement was signed on February 12, 1953 without invitation of or at least reference to Southern opinion.

Lastly, the decision of the Sudanese Council of Ministers in June 1954 for immediate Sudanization of the Equatoria Corps, despite warnings of the Commanding Officer of difficulties that such a step could cause. In other words, whereas Sudanization of the Southern Sudan should have taken place over several years (at least due to the lack of sufficient administrative personnel) it was still possible in June 1954 to have expected at least two to three years handover. The Council's decision had shown either complete irresponsibility or total ignorance of the political discontent in or/and the true feelings in the South.54

The result was administrative meddling, which had further heightened the political tensions that culminated in the August 1955 rebellion.

End Notes

1   Takhrir Lajnat Tahkik al-Idari---, pp. 1-15, K.D.D. Henderson, *The Sudan Republic*, (London: Ernest Benn Limited, 1965), pp. 170-71; London: House of Commons, *Parliamentary Debates* 7th December 1955, pp. 57-58.
2   Takhrir Lajnat Tahkik al-Idari, pp. 1-5.
3   Ibid., pp. 1-2.
4   Ibid., pp. 1-2.
5   Ibid., pp. 1-5.
6   Takhrir Lajnat Tahkik al-Idari---, pp. 1-2.
7   Keith Kyle, "The Southern Problem in the Sudan" *The World Today* 22 (1966), pp. 512-520.
8   Takhrir Lajnat al-Idari---, pp. 1-5; also see Beshir Mohammed Said, *The Sudan: Crossroads of Africa*, (London: The Bodley Head, 1965), pp. 32-35; also see Muddathir Abdel Rahim, "The Development of British Policy on the Southern Sudan, 1899-1947" *Middle Eastern Studies* 2, 3 (April 1966), pp. 227-229.
9   Takhrir Lajnat Tahkik al-Idari---, pp. 1-5; also see Raphael K. Badal, "The Rise and

The End of the Mutiny

Fall of Separatism in Southern Sudan" *African Affairs* 75, 301 (October 1976), pp. 463-474; also see Abdel Rahim, "The Development of British Policy in the Southern Sudan, 1899-1947". pp. 227-249; for more details see Henderson, *The Sudan Republic*, pp. 162-169. Also see John Howell, "Politics in Southern Sudan" *African Affairs* 72 (April 1973), pp. 163-178.

10 See Takrir Lajnat Tahkik al-Idari, p. 95. N. Manfred Shaffer, "The Sudan: Arab-African Confrontation" *Current History* (March 1966), pp. 142-146/178; also said, *The Sudan: Crossroads of AFrica*, pp. 35-36.

11 Takhrir Lajnat Tahkik al-Idari, pp. 6-9. J.W. Kenrik, "The Reminiscences around the Transfer of Power in the Sudan" in *The Condomium Remmbered: The Making of the Sudanese State*, Vol. 1, edited by Deborah Levin, (Durham: University of Durham, 1991), pp. 157-164.

12 Lilian M.P. Sanderson and G.N. Sanderson, *Education, Religion and Politics in Southern Sudan, 1899-1964*, (London: Ithaca press, 1981), pp. 325-351; also see Peter R. Woodward, "The South in Sudan Politics, 1946-1956" *Middle Eastern Studies* 16 (1980), pp. 178-92. Throughout the year 1955, the Egyptian media especially 'Radio Cairo' and Al-Aharam newspapers have attacked al-Azhari, for having changed from pro-Egyptian resolute to a pro-independence pioneer. See *Al-Aharam* 25 July 1955, p. 4; *Rose al-Youssef* 14 November 1955, p. 8; and *Rose al-Youssef* 18 July 1955, pp. 3-4 and *Al-Musawwar* 26 August 1955, p. 10.

13 On the role of major Salah Salim see *Al-Aharam*, 28 July 1955, pp. 1 and 9; and *Al-Aharam*, 12 August 1955, pp. 1 and 8; also refer to Sanderson, *Education, Religion and Politics in Southern Sudan*, pp. 341-346. *Among the leading Southern politicians who became outspoken against unity of the South with Egypt were Stanislaus Pasayema, Both Diu, Siricio Iro, Benjamin Lowki, Buller Alier and others.

14 Martin W. Daly, "Broken bridge and empty basket, The Political and Economic Background of the Sudaense Civil War" in *Civil War in the Sudan*, edited by M.W. Daly and Ahmed A. Sikainga (London: British Academic Press, 1993), pp. 1-27; see *Al-Aharam*, 7 August 1955, p. 7.

15 See *Al-Aharam* (Cairo) 28 July 1955, pp. 1 & 9; also Woodward, "The South in the Sudanese Politics", pp. 178-90; also see Trevelyan, *The Middle East in Revolution*, pp. 15-25.

16 For more details see *Al-Hayat* (Beirut), September 4, 1955, pp. 1 and 7; *Al-Aharam*, (Cairo) August 5, 1955, pp. 1 and 13; also refer to *Al-Hayat* (Beirut) 30 August, 1955, pp. 1 and 8. * In addition to 'Radio Cairo', *Al-Aharam* and *Rose El-Yousef* had conducted interviews with Southern politicians.

17 Takrir Lajnat Tahkik al-Idari fi Hawadith al-Junub----, p. 113. * The name "Anti-Imperial Front" was the official name of the Sudan Communist Party, which the government recognized soon after the independence.

18 Ibid., p. 114.
19 Dustan M. Wai, *The African-Arab Conflict in the Sudan*, (New York: Africana Publishing Company, 1981), p. 63.
20 See Takhrir Lajnat Tahkik al-Idari, p. 114. John Howell, "Politics in the Southern Sudan" *African Affairs* 72, 287 (April 1973), pp. 163-78; also see Takrir Lajinat Tahkik al Idari----, p. 114.
21 Henderson, *The Sudan Republic,* pp. 171-83.
22 Takhrir Lajnat Tahkik al-Idari---, pp. 128-140. Also see David Sconyers, "Hurrying Home: Sudanization and National Integration, 1953-1956" *British Society for Middle Eastern Studies Bulletin* 15, 192 (1988), pp. 64-74; also Said, *The Sudan: Crossroads of Africa,* p. 77.
23 Sconyers, "Hurrying Home: Sudanization and National Integration, 1953-1956", pp. 64-74; for more details refer to P.B. Browbent, "Sudanese Self-Government" *International Affairs* 30(1954), pp. 320-330; also see Takhrir Lajnat Tahkik al-Idari--, pp. 128-129.
24 Mohammed Omer Beshir, *The Southern Sudan: Background to Conflict,* (Khartoum: Khartoum University Press, 1970), pp. 70-72; also see *Al-Aharam* (Cairo), 13 August 1955, pp. 6 and 13; Takhrir Lajnat Tahkik al-Idari---, p. 132.
25 Sir James Robertson, "The Sudan in Transition" *African Affairs* 52, 209 (October 1953), pp. 317-27; also Martin W. Daly, *Imperial Sudan: The Anglo-Egyptian Condominium, 1934-1956,* (Cambridge: Cambridge University Press, 1991), pp. 378-382.
26 L.t. Col. W.B.E. Brown, "Some Reminiscences and personal views concerning the Sudanization of the Equatorial Corps, in 1954" in *The Condominium Remembered: The making of the Sudanese State,* Vol. 9, (Durham: Centre for Middle Eastern and Islamic Studies, University of Durham, 1991), pp. 141-143; also see Sam C. Sarkesian, "The Southern Sudan: A Reassessment" *African Studies Review* 16 (1973), pp. 1-20.
27 Robert O. Collins, *Shadows in the Grass: Britain in the Southern Sudan, 1918-1956,* (New Haven: Yale University Press, 1983), pp. 443-456; also see Daly, *Imperial Sudan,* 378-380.
28 Wai, *The African-Arab Conflict in the Sudan,* p. 56.
29 Oliver Albino,, *The Sudan: A Southern Viewpoint,* (London: Oxford University Press, 1970), p. 33.
30 Said, *The Sudan: Crossroads of Africa,* p. 74.
31 Beshir, *The Southern Sudan: Background to Conflict,* pp. 72-73.
32 Dustan M. Wai, "Political Trends in the Sudan and the Future of the South" in *The Southern Sudan: The Problem of National Integration,* edited by Dustan M.

The End of the Mutiny

Wai, (London: Frank Cass and Company Limited, 1973), pp. 145-70; also see Henderson, *The Sudan Republic*, pp. 171-83; Takhrir Lajnat Tahkik al-Idari---, pp. 130-31.

33 Daly, *Imperial Sudan*, pp. 382-88; see also Tahkrir Lajnat Tahkik Al-Idari.
34 Takhrir Lajnat Tahkik al-Idari ---, p. 23.
35 Peter R. Woodward, *The Sudan, 1898-1989: The Unstable State*, (London: Lester Grook Academic Publishing, 1990), pp. 88-91.
36 Sconyers, "Hurrying Home---", pp. 64-74; also see Sanderson, *Education, Religion and Politics in Southern Sudan*, pp. 338-346.
37 George W. Shepherd Jr., "National Integration and the Southern Sudan" *Journal of Modern African Studies* 4, 2 (1966), pp. 193-212; also refer to Collins, *Shadows in the Grass*, pp. 443-456.
38 Tahkrir Lajinat Tahkik al-Idari---, p. 131.
39 Wai, *African-Arab Conflict in the Sudan*, p. 58; the full text of the alleged telegram is also found in *Al-Aharam*, 5 August 1955, pp. 1 and 13; also see Takhrir Lajnat Tahkik al-Idari---, p. 96.
40 Tahkrir Lajnat Tahkik al-Idari ---, pp. 96-106.
41 Edgar O'Ballance, *The Secret War in the Sudan: 1955-1972*, (Hamden Connecticut: Archon Books, 1977), p. 40; also see Blanka Richova, "Ethnic Conflict as the Factor of State Coherency in Africa: The Case of the Sudan" *Archiv Orietnalni* 59 (1991), pp. 289-312; see Takhrir Lajnat Tahkik al-Idari---, pp. 96-102.
42 Tahkrir Lajinat Tahkik al-Idari---, pp. 106-112.
43 This alleged telegram was also attacked by some Southern politicians who were in Cairo on an official visit, see *Al-Ahram*, (Cairo), 6 August 1955, pp. 6 and 8. Also see Wai, *African-Arab Conflict in the Sudan*, p. 62.
44 Tahkrir Lajinat Tahkik al-Idari---, p. 107. *The Cotran Report identified the two merchants who shot at the crowd as Mohammed Ali, and Abas Hassoun; see Takhrir Lajnat Tahkik al-Idari, p. 118.
45 Ibid., pp. 110-111.
46 Cecil Eprile, *War and Peace in the Sudan; 1955-1972*, (London: David and Charles, 1974), pp. 40-41; also see O'Ballance, *The Secret War in the Sudan*, p. 46; Takhrir Lajnat Tahkik al-Idari---, pp. 104-105.
47 Tahkrir Lajinat Tahkik al-Idari---, pp. 116-120.
48 Ibid., pp. 116-119.
49 Tahkrir Lajnat Tahkik al-Idari---, pp. 119-121. Peter Rusell and Storrs Mc Call, "Can Secessioin be justified? The Case of the Southern Sudan" in *The Southern Sudan: The Problem of National Integration* edited by Dustan M. Wai, pp. 91-121.

50 Henderson, *The Sudan Republic,* pp. 171-83; Takhrir Lajnat Tahkik al-Idari---, p. 8.
51 Eprile, *War and Peace in the Sudan,* pp. 45-47. * *Gallaba* is the name used by Southerners when referring to Northern traders in the South, Takhrir Lajnat Tahkik al-Idari---, p. 146.
52 Henderson, *The Sudan Republic*, p. 178; Takhrir Lajnat Tahkik al-Idari---, pp. 145-148.
53 Takhrir Lajnat Tahkik al_Idari fi Hawadith al-Junub al-Sudan, (Khartoum, Feb. 1956), pp. 1-5. *The two parties tend to blame each other when dealing with socio-economic aspects of post-independent administration; however, they do agree on the British short-comings during the colonial rule. On Egyptian point of view regarding the causes of the mutiny see *al-Masawwar*, 16 August 1955, pp. 12-13.

CHAPTER FOUR

The Torit Mutiny and its Impact on National Politics

It is often held that the outbreak of the Torit mutiny was responsible for the subsequent deterioration of the North-South relations in the 1960's. In fact most of the Southern politicians, who were to form the leadership of the Southern militant organizations in exile, were either imprisoned or suspected of involvement in the mutiny. The investigation of their activities in post Torit mutiny politics is therefore of great significance for better understanding of the impact the mutiny had had on the national politics. Therefore, the evolution of the Torit mutiny into what was known as 'Southern problem' can be understood within the context North-South relations after the mutiny.[1]

There is no doubt that the formation of Southern militant groups in exile had transformed the North-South political relations into direct military confrontation. The evolution of the Torit mutineers into an effective fighting force can therefore be considered responsible for the delay of peaceful solution to the Southern problem. Moreover, the weakness of subsequent coalition governments in the North in the 1960's had also contributed negatively in solving the problem through democratic and constitutional means. Most of the Northern political groups lacked at the time a concrete and a unified vision of how the problem could be solved.²

One of the major negative repercussions of the Torit Mutiny on Sudanese national politics, was that it almost paralyzed effective political dialogue between the Southern Sudanese political groups and the central government, as well as casting doubt on the credibility of the Liberal Party and its members. This state of affairs was clearly manifested when the final phase of negotiations on independence between the Condominium authorities and the Sudanese political groups were resumed in October 1955. Southern politicians found themselves powerless and unable to manoeuvre or to push through the least of their demands. Put differently, their alleged linkage to the mutiny leadership, and their alleged alliance with Major Salah Salim, had become a real political impediment on the eve of the independence.³

It is generally accepted that the Southern region of the Sudan as a political "interest group" had started first as a reformist party, demanding among other things, rapid economic and educational development, before any decision could be taken on its political future. When this demand was not fulfilled, the South shifted to demand a federal status so as to avoid future political and administrative problems between the North and the South.⁴ Committed to achieve federal status for the South, a group of Southern intellectuals, in December 1953, decided to form a political party which they named Southern Liberal Party'. The founders of the Southern Liberal party, as it later became known, were Benjamin Langjuk, Both Diu, Alfred Burjuok, Clement Mboro, Gordon Ayoum, Abdel Rahman Sule, Stanislaus Peysama and Benjamin Lwoke.⁵

The Torit Mutiny and its Impact on National Politics

By January 1954, the Liberal Party had become a leading Sudanese party opposed to the National Unionist Party, NUP, which was in control of the government. The first Liberal party conference, which was attended by a bout 200 delegates, was held in Juba Hall on 18th October 1954. On the fourth day the conferees resolved: "that Southern peoples stand firmly for full independence and that a note would be prepared for submission to the Condominium authorities on Federal lines for a United Sudan."[6] Indeed a letter to this effect was sent to the Condominium authority.

As pointed out earlier the results of the Sudanization Committee were published in October 1954, and the liberals threatened to boycott the national politics until something was done about the results.[7] However, nothing was done about the commission report, nor did the Liberals execute their threat. In January 1955, the Liberal party, together with the Southern members of the NUP, held a second conference, again in Juba, in which they advocated an independent parliament for the South in a form of federal relations with Egypt and the Northern Sudan. Again, a third secret Liberal Party conference was convened on 5th-6th July 1955, in Juba in which federalism and the possibility of "use of violence against al-Azhari government" was discussed.[8]

However, when the Torit Mutiny broke out on 18th August, the Liberal party denied any involvement of its leadership. In fact, the Secretary General, Both Diu said that although he was concerned about the impending anti-Northern violence in the South, he felt helpless to do anything to stop it. Later on the party leader, Stanislaus Peysama recalled that while in Wau, he was warned that if the Southern parliamentarians returned to Khartoum for the new session, beginning on 18th August 1955, they would face violent action.⁹

Despite the lack of direct evidence implicating the Liberal party leadership, a considerable number of them were detained in three Southern provinces; they included Clement Mboro, Elia Kuze, Stanislaus Peysama and many others.¹⁰ The ten-man delegation which was appointed by the Liberal party's July 1955 conference to present its views to the Northern parties in Khartoum, did not present their memorandum as the Torit rebellion took place in August.¹¹

Reporting on the situation in the Southern Sudan a few weeks after the mutiny, Collin Legum wrote:

> The Southern MPs (Liberal Partisans) have not visited their constituencies since the troubles began. Whatever the cause it seems probable that they lost the confidence of their constituents and it is questionable whether they are in a position to express the feelings of the South on the major issues that will arise.¹²

The major issues referred to by *The Times* correspondent were the impending negotiations concerning the independence of the country. In fact, the Liberal party's activities were drastically limited in the aftermath of the Torit insurrection. Internally, changes in the leadership of the Liberal party took place. Alfred Burjuok took over from Both Diu as Secretary General and Benjamin Lwoke replaced Stanislaus Peysama as President of the party. In November 1955, in his capacity as the leader of the Southern Liberal party, Lwoke wrote to Prime Minister Al-Azhari, informing him that the liberals could not accept that the present parliament have the legitimacy to decide the country's future while there was still unrest in the South. His memorandum was ignored by the Umma party and the NUP, who had already reached an agreement to go ahead with independence.[13]

On 18th December, Lwoke, along with others, were invited by the Northern parties to attend a meeting in which parts of the proposed draft motion for independence would be discussed. The parts of the motion in question were the ones that would permit a future constituent Assembly to give consideration to federalism. It is probable that most of the Southern leaders at the time were genuine believers in a federal status for the South. Yet, for others who were in favour of an independent South, a federation could have created a balance of power, which, they hoped, could have facilitated the transformation of the South from a federal to an independent state without much loss of lives on either side. It was perhaps on those grounds that the Liberal party accepted the independence of a united Sudan.[14]

On 19th December 1955, the parliament unanimously adopted an independence motion and resolved that:

> ...the claims of the Southern members of parliament for a federal government for the three Southern provinces be given full consideration by the Constituent Assembly."[15]

The Northern political groups had therefore, agreed to consider a federal solution for the Sudan, and hence, on the strength of this promise, the Liberal party's votes gave the resolution its credible and totally effective unanimity.

In other words, the North was understood by Southern parliamentarians to have made a pledge to work for some sort of federal relationship as a safeguard against what the South considered to be "cultural assimilation, the monopoly of policy-making, of jobs, social services and economic development plans".[16]

What the Southern Liberal party considered to be 'a gentleman's agreement' meant in practice forwarding the idea of federalism to the constitutional commission, which as promised, was to be appointed by the Constituent Assembly. Indeed, the parliament did appoint in September 1956, a national constitutional committee composed of 46 members, three of whom were from the South. The 43 Northern members opted for a strong, centralized and unitary system of government. Their Southern counterparts called for a federal constitution. The Northern members in the committee turned down federation on the basis that it was not feasible. Unable to convince the other forty three members of the committee, the three Southern Members decided to boycott the meetings of the constitutional committee.[17] However, their withdrawal did not stop the work of the committee which continued its deliberations and later on submitted its recommendations to the parliament in June 1958.

The withdrawal of the Southern Members from the committee revealed the Liberal party's inability to influence the committee. In part its weakness arose from the divisions among its leadership, which in practice meant that Southern ministers were appointed and often dismissed and different factions were formed and

The Torit Mutiny and its Impact on National Politics

dissolved without concrete justifications. A more significant cause was that the party did not have membership lists*, constitution, or a bank account of its own. Added to these, there were no party premises in any of the provincial branches.

Informal meetings of the party were held at homes and in officials' clubs. The most serious problem however, was the leadership rivalry between Benjamin Lwoke and Stanislaus Peysama, which had frustrated several Southern politicians and led some of them to join Northern parties.[18] The last schism came in May 1957, when over half of the party members elected Peysama as the new President. Lwoke's faction reacted by calling for a meeting in which he formed his own executive committee. As later developments would show, the rivalry between the two men was irreconcilable; none of the two leaders was able to establish his authority when the 1958 elections approached.[19]

It was because of the absence of trust among Southern politicians that Ezboni Mundiri, then a young graduate of Khartoum University, decided, a long with others, to form a new party, which he called the Federal Party. The formation of the Federal Party introduced a new factor in Southern politics; a more radical group was now actively involved in challenging the Liberal Party's virtual political hegemony. On 30th June 1957, parliament was dissolved in preparation for elections, which indeed took place from 27th February to 9th March 1958. Of the 46 seats allocated to the South, 36 were new to the parliament. Most of the old Liberal party leadership lost their parliamentary seats. Benjamin Lwoke lost his seat; Alfred Burjuok and Philemon Majok, both former Liberal ministers, lost in Bhar El-Ghazal Province. Only Both

Diu and Stanislaus Peysama retained their seats. The results thus contributed to the emergence of a new radical Southern leadership.[20]

The new federalists grouped themselves into "a federal parliamentary Bloc". The Bloc, under the leadership of Fr. Saturnino Lohure, incorporated what remained of the Liberal party, Peysama became the patron; Lohure President, Elija Mayoum Vice President and Luigi Adwok, Secretary General. The first task, which was awaiting the federalists was the discussion of the Federal Constitution which they hoped, would be passed by the new parliament.

The 43 members of the September 1956 constitutional committee had completed and submitted their draft report to the new parliament in May 1958. They recommended, among other things, that:
- The Sudan should become a unitary parliamentary democratic republic,
- Islam should become the country's official state religion
- Arabic should become the official and national language.

The federalists rejected these recommendations and realizing that they were not influencing the debate, they walked out of the Assembly.[21] With the Southern MPs out of the House, the Northern MPs then decided to submit the draft report to a 40 member parliamentary committee for study and for the submission of a report not later then 17th November 1958.[22]

Following several informal meetings between Northern and Southern parliamentarians, Southern MPs were persuaded to return to the constituent Assembly, in order to explain their view regarding the draft constitution. This view was summarized in the following extract from the speech delivered by Fr. Saturnino Lohure, before the parliament on 16th June 1958:

> Mr. President Sir, the South has no ill-intentions whatsoever towards the North; the South simply claims to run its local affairs in a United Sudan. The South has no intention of separating from the North for had that been the case nothing on earth could have prevented the demand for separation. The South claims to Federate with the North, a right that the South undoubtedly possesses as a consequence of the principle of free self-determination, which reason and democracy grant to a free people. The South will at any moment separate from the North if and when the North so desires, directly or indirectly, through political, social and economic subjection of the South."[23]

It was therefore during this period of uncertainty in the country that the Army took over on November 17th, 1958. With General Ibrahim Abboud ascendancy to power, the South-north political dialogue entered a new phase.

Despite its shortcomings, the experience of the parliamentary system in the Sudan seemed to have had two positive consequences:[24]

Parliamentary politics had helped to restrain Northern hardliners who wished to suppress Southern partisans who had openly called for federation or separation.

It did provide a free forum for continuing a peaceful dialogue between the leaders of the two regions in an attempt to reach an honest and realistic compromise.

The Sudanese short-lived parliamentary experience represented therefore the politics of compromise in which, cooperation, and not confrontation, was the norm.[25] In other words, although these first three years of independence were essentially barren as regards the question of the South, nevertheless, politicians were able to meet and freely discuss ways to resolve the dilemma. With the military take over, however a new type of politics emerged not in Khartoum, but this time in exile.

The Sudan African National Union (SANU)

The ascendancy of the military to power drastically transformed the North-South political dialogue from that of cooperation to confrontation; and by mid 1959, the legacy of the Torit revolt resurfaced on the national political scene. In December 1960, a plan to carry out a mass arrest of Southern MPs and politicians was revealed. To avoid imminent arrests, several Southern politicians, many of them having just been released from prison, decided to leave the country to the neighbouring countries bordering Sudan. The first group to leave for East Africa were Elia Lupe, Joseph H. Oduho, Fr. Saturnino Lohure, Ferdinand Adyang, William Deng Nhial and Samuel Renzi.

In 1962 another group fled the country, among them were Dominic Murwell and Ezboni Mundiri. Those of them who had

The Torit Mutiny and its Impact on National Politics

settled in East Africa, made efforts to mobilize Southern University students abroad to help in propagating what they described as the Southern cause. These efforts bore fruit especially among those students who had gained church scholarships in England. Those students who accepted to take on new responsibility were Philip Pedak Lieth, Natale Olwak and George Kwanai, all of who were to become influential in the Southern politics in exile.[26]

Using Leopoldville, Zaire, as their headquarters, some Southern exiles formed in February 1962, a new political organization, which they called "The Sudan Closed Districts National Union", SACDNU. Fr. Saturnino Lohure became the organization's Patron, Oduho was its President, Marko Rume, its Vice President, William Deng Nhial, its Secretary General and Aggrey Jaden became the Assistant Secretary General. The new organization was different in many expects from traditional Southern organizations as they existed prior to the military take over. For one, it linked itself to the Torit mutiny soldiers who were in hiding inside Southern Sudan bushes since August 1955. It was also militant in character; and its main goal was to liberate Southern Sudan from the Sudanese Central government hegemony, and to establish an independent sovereign state.[27]

In order to preach its new politics, the SACDNU leadership had to use Rome and London as the starting points, where both finance and media accesses were provided by their contacts there. In London for instance, the SACDNU leadership began publication of the movement's newsletter *Voice of the Southern Sudan* in March 1963. Again, it was in London that Joseph H. Oduho and William Deng Nhial managed to persuade the Institute of Race Relations to accept the SACDNU statement of policy for publication entitled *The Problem of the Southern Sudan*.[28]

Having managed to establish the movement's mouthpiece, the leadership decided in October 1963 to rename SACDNU to become the Sudan African National Union or SANU. Many attempts were made to use Uganda as the organization's base since it was closer to Southern Sudan but the Ugandan authorities found themselves caught between cross-pressures. On the one hand it wanted to help the South Sudanese political exiles, but it also wanted to maintain good relations with its neighbour, the Sudan. Thus, in October 1963, Joseph Oduho, the SANU leader, and several others were detained, but later released, by the Ugandan government for running an unofficial organization on its territory and for organizing attacks against the Sudan.[29]

The October Uprising

Judging by the absence of reported violence, the military regime seemed to have apparently experienced little difficulties in the South, apart from some sporadic Anya Nya attacks on police posts. However, the period of military rule was notable not only for awakening Southern politicians to engage in serious political work in exile, and indeed inside the country, but also because it witnessed the replacement of the old set of political leaders by new ones inside and outside the country.[30]

Convinced that coercion was pointless, the military government decided in September 1964 to appoint a Commission of Inquiry. The

The Torit Mutiny and its Impact on National Politics

Commission was to investigate the causes of unrest in the South and to make recommendations with the intention of achieving internal stability in the country. The formation of the commission was seen as an indirect confession of the government's failure to restore confidence both in the North and in the South.31 The appointment of the Commission was also seen as a beginning of a long awaited decision to open up a dialogue to explore ways and means to find a peaceful solution to the problem of the South.

The general political atmosphere in the country during the military rule, was best described by Robert Collins who wrote:

By 1962, however, numerous urban elements, including the intelligensia, the trade unions, and civil servants, as well as the powerful religious brotherhoods, the Turuq, had become bored and dischanted with the military regime.... Even the conservative religious brotherhoods grew restless when they were unable to carry on their former political activities. Moreover, the tribal masses and growing proletariat had become increasingly apathetic toward the government, for even if the parliamentarians were corrupt, they were at least exciting and colorful. Military reviews, parades, and heroic pronouncements were no substitute for the enthusiasm generated by party politics and the passions stirred by political action. The military government never provided an outlet for the political frustrations of the Sudanese, and, in the end, the regime was overwhelmed by boredom and overthrown by the reaction to its lassitude. The means, not the cause, was the Southern Sudan.[32]

On October 21, 1964, an open debate at Khartoum University on the Southern problem triggered off a series of demonstrations in the capital. The demonstrations gradually developed into a general popular uprising, and it included businessmen, government civil servants, old traditional parties with their veteran leaders and other organizations.

Grouping themselves into National Front, the traditional political parties and newly formed Leftist and Islamist organizations demanded, among other things:
- Withdrawal of the army from power,
- Immediate resignation of the government;
- The restoration of the 1956 constitution
- Resolution to the problem of the South.

The army did hand over power on the third day of the uprising after a student and two other demonstrators were killed and over a hundred injured. A week later an interim government was installed.[33]

Challenges of the Southern Organizations

Much of the Southern Sudanese political life in exile seemed to have been characterized by lack of any form of organizational structure through which divisions among its antagonizing leadership could be resolved. Most Southern parties and movements did not have constitutions or if they were available, they lacked any prospect of enforceability. Internal divisions, at one point, had developed into

The Torit Mutiny and its Impact on National Politics

a phenomenon of creating a series of political movements each claiming to represent the Southern separatist movement.

First of all, for different reasons, SANU and its successors did not have party offices or formal meeting-places, nor were the various Fronts, Councils and Provisional or revolutionary governments bureaucratized. In fact, these organizations remained largely informal groups of friends or political allies, subject of course, to the hardship of the political life of exiles.[34]

Secondly, almost all the Southern politicians in exile were often in financial difficulties. Regulations governing financial accountability were non-existent or at least had proven ineffective. This could be explained by the fact that many organizational efforts were intentionally opposed as individual politicians were often ready to give up politics.

Thirdly, there were no mechanisms for regulating policies, decision or solving questions relating to leadership and responsibility. Therefore, without agreed principles, Southern political organizations, both within and without the Sudan, were characterized by a high degree of individualism; this conduct led to arbitrary dismissals based of course, on no accepted convention or rule.

Finally, external financial aid and its distribution generated great resentment owing to the lack of official channels for controlling expenditure.[35] This element of mistrust among Southern politicians, caused continuous floor-crossing among individual Southern politicians who felt excluded from privileges of office and from benefiting financially. This was the case among some individuals who had no independent source of income. All these shortcomings had their negative effect on the South-North relations and it was difficult for the central government to make peace with such fragmented political groups.

Regarding the Southern politicians within the country, their situation was more or less similar to the one discussed above. In fact, political patronage among them was an important means of acquiring a post. It is generally agreed that many Southern intellectuals aspired to hold one important post or another. In this case ethnicity or ethnic background was of great importance.[36] Put differently, one's closeness to the Northern ruling party was an important asset, as was the strength of one's ethnic base. Patronage in the North depended on the manner in which each political party viewed the Southern problem.

For example, the importance and the impact of Southern elite in the national politics was viewed by the Northern politicians in three different perspectives:

That Southerners should be given independence and left to sort out the problems of governing themselves. This view was held by the Muslim brothers or the "National Islamic Charter" as they were known.[37]

Secondly, that they should be treated as self-seeking trouble makers from the "missionaries schools" unrepresentative of Southerners, should be excluded from politics, and if necessary suppressed. This view was perceived and propagated by the Umma party.

That they should be brought into government, given posts of authority, especially in their own region; and they must be encouraged to remain an integral part of the Sudan.[38] This view was propagated by the Sudan Communist party.

The Torit Mutiny and its Impact on National Politics

End Notes

1 Wai, *The African-Arab Conflict in the Sudan*, pp. 67-90.
2 O'Ballance, *The Secret War in the Sudan*, pp. 44-50.
3 Sam C. Sarkesian, "The Southern Sudan: A Reassessment," *African Studies Review*, 16 (1973), pp. 1 - 22; also see Muhammad Abu Al-Qasim Hajj Hamad. *Al-Sudan: Al Ma'ziq Al-Tarikhi Wa Afaq Al-Mustaqbal* (Beirut: Dar Al-Kalima Lil Nashr, 1980), pp. 373-413; Ibrahim Ahmed Al-Adawi. *Yaqzat Al-Sudan* (Cairo: Makatabat Anglo-Inqlizi Al-Masri, 1956), pp. 124-133.
4 See Jamil Ilyas Afara, *Mustaqbal Al-Sudan Al-Siyasi* (Beirut: Sharikat Al-Tiba'a Wa Al-Nashr Al Lubnaniyya, 1958), pp. 118-125; also see Al-Adawi, *Yaqzat Al-Sudan*, pp. 108-143.
5 Blanka Richova Praha, "The Ethnic Conflict as the Factor of State Coherency in Africa: The Case of the Sudan," *Archiv Orientalni*, 59 (1991), pp. 289-312; more details are given by Henderson, *Sudan Republic*, pp. 171-174; also see Beshir, *The Southern Sudan: Background to Conflict*, pp. 73-74; Howell, "Political Leadership and Organization in the Southern Sudan" (Reading: University of Reasing, PhD dissert., 1978), pp. 121-126.
6 Lilian P. Sanderson and Neville Sanderson, *Education, Religion and Politics in Southern Sudan 1899-1964* (London: Ithaca press, 1981), pp. 340-342.
7 Takrir Lajnat Tahkik al-Idari, pp. 96-106.
8 Albino, *The Sudan: A Southern Viewpoint*, pp. 34-36; Howell, "Political Leadership", pp. 123-126; also see Joseph Oduho and William Deng, *The Problem of the Southern Sudan* (London: Oxford University Press, 1963), pp. 26-28.
9 The Liberal Party's view of the Torit Mutiny, especially the alleged involvement of the party is discussed in Oduho, *The Problem of the Southern Sudan*, pp. 28-31.
10 O'Ballence, *The Secret War in the Sudan*, pp. 40-43; also see Howell, "Political Leadership", pp. 133-137.
11 Sanderson, *Education, Religion and Politics in Southern Sudan*, pp. 341-343.
12 *The Times* (London), 27 October 1955.
13 Wai, *The AFrican-Arab Conflict in the Sudan*, pp. 68-70.
14 Albino, *The Sudan: A Southern Viewpoint*, pp. XIII-XIV; also see Wai, *The African-Arab Conflict in the Sudan*, pp. 70-77.
15 Abel Alier, *Southern Sudan: Too Many Agreements Dishonoured* (Exter: Ithaca Press, 1990), pp. 22-23; more details on Federal discussion are given by Daly, *Imperial Sudan*, pp. 391-394.

16 Abdel Wahab El-Affendi, "Discovering the South: Sudanese Dilemmas for Islam in Africa," *African Affairs*, 89 (July 1990), pp. 371-389; also Abel Alier, "The Southern Sudan Quesiton," in *The Southern Sudan: The Problem of National Integration*, edited by Dustan M. Wai, (London: Frank Cass, Ltd., 1973), pp. 11-27.

17 Beshir M. Said, *The Sudan Crossroads of Africa*, pp. 82-84; also see Francis Mading Deng, "War of Visions for the Nation," *Middle East Journal*, 44, 4 (1990), pp. 591-609; *Membership to the Liberal party was restricted to the intellectuals and their immediate associates such as students, police and army officers. Tribal headmen were also considered partisans because of their influence in villages during elections.

18 Deng Awur Wenyin, *Southern Sudan and The Making of a Permanent Constitution in Sudan* (Khartoum: University of Juba, 1987), pp. 3-30; also see Howell, "Political Leadership", pp. 177-181.

19 Howell, "Political Leadership", p. 163.

20 Ibid., pp. 166-169.

21 Abdullahi Ahmed An Naim, "Constitutional Discourse and the Civil War in the Sudan" in *Civil War in the Sudan*, edited by M.W. Daly and Ahmed A. Sikeinga (London: British Academic press, 1993), pp. 97-116; also see Beshir, *Southern Sudan: Background to Conflict*, pp. 78-79.

22 Thomas Graham, *udan 1950-1985: Death of A Dream*, (London: Darf Publishers, Ltd., 1990), pp. 81-103; Russell and McCall "Can Secession be Justified? The Case of the Sudan", pp. 99-121.

23 Wai, *The African-Arab Conflict in Sudan*, pp. 71-77, also Wenyin, *Southern Sudan and The Making of a Permanent Constitution*, p. 14.

24 Elias N. Wakoson, "The Origins and Development of the AnyaNya Movement 1955-1972" in *Southern Sudan: Regionalism and Religion*, edited by Mohamed O. Beshir (Khartoum: University of Khartoum, 1984), pp. 172-174.

25 On the mass exodus of the Southern Sudanese politicians to East Africa see Oduho, *The Problem of Southern Sudan*, pp. 40-42; Wai, *African-Arab Conflict in the Sudan*, pp. 89-92; Wakoson, "The Origins and Development of the AnyaNya Movement", pp. 179-180.

26 N. Manfred Shaffer, "The Sudan: Arab-African Confrontation," *Current History* (March 1966), pp. 142-146/178; also Keith Kyle, "The Southern Problem in the Sudan, *The World Today* 22 (1966), pp. 512-520.

27 Howell, "Political Leadership", p. 191.

28 Wakoson, "The Origin and Development of the AnyaNya Movement", pp. 127-204.

29 Wai, *The African-Arab Conflict in the Sudan*, pp. 110-115; Wakoson, "The Origin and Development of the AnyaNya Movement", pp. 127-155. *The word "AnyaNya"

is said to be a Lotuko version of the term *InyaNya,* which in Madi and Moru languages means "The venom of the Gabon Viber".

30 Alier, *Southern Sudan: Too Many Agreements,* p. 25.

31 Robert O. Collins, "The Sudan: Link to the North," *The Transformation of East Africa,* edited by Stanley Diamond and Fred G. Berke (New York: Basic Books, 1966), pp. 1-2.

32 Hassan, "The Sudanese Revolution of October 1964", pp. 491-509; Hajj Hamad, *Al-Sudan: Al-Ma'ziq Al-Tarikhi Wa Afaq Al-Mustaqbal,* pp. 375-413.

34 Holt, *A History of the Sudan,* pp. 186-191; also Wai, *African-Arab Conflict in the Sudan,* p. 98.

35 John O. Voll and Sarah P. Voll, *The Sudan: Unity and Diversity in a Multicultural State* (Boulder, Colo.: Westview Press, 1985), pp. 75-78; Beshir, *Southern Sudan, Background to Conflict,* pp. 88-97.

36 Kyle, "The Sudan Today", pp. 233-244.

37 Kyle, "The Southern Problem in the Sudan", pp. 512-520; Albino, *The Sudan: A Southern Viewpoint,* pp. 56-60;

38. Beshir, *outhern Sudan: Background to Conflict,* pp. 165-186, Alier, *Southern Sudan,* pp. 29-40;; see also Raphael K. Badal, "The Rise and Fall of Separation in Southern Sudan," *African Affairs,* 75 (October 1976), pp. 463-474.

CHAPTER FIVE

The Rise and the Development of the Anyanya Movement *

The National Liberation Army or the Anya Nya, was officially established on 18th August 1963, the date which marked the eighth anniversary of the Torit Mutiny. The proclamation announcing the creation of what later became the military wing of SANU, was released in Kampala, Uganda. An Any aNya General acknowledged SANU's efforts to find a peaceful solution to the Southern Sudanese problem. But he went on to say:

> ...(O)ur patience has now come to an end, and we are convinced that only use of force will bring a decision...from today onwards we shall take action for better or for worse – we do not want mercy and we are not prepared to give it.¹

The newly proclaimed Anya Nya force chose to fight for the liberation of the Southern Sudan from North, with the ultimate aim of establishing a sovereign African state. The new rebel movement was composed mainly of Torit Mutiny regulars who had gone into the bushes of the Southern Sudan, and of soldiers of the same mutiny who had taken up jobs in East Africa.

The Rise and the Development of the Anyanya Movement

In the initial stages, the force was poorly armed; however, it did have some well-trained defected officers who had some skills of guerilla warfare tactics and who had deserted the ranks of the regular Sudanese army.[2] In the opening stages of its activities the Anya Nya resistance tended to be geographically and ethnically based where each ethnic group operated in the area. Keen on their newly acquired authority, these guerillas were resentful of civilians and politicians alike. In fact, the politicians and later on some senior AnyaNya leaders, had to give in and accept the Anya Nya as the only effective military wing of the Southern Sudan movement.[3] This in practice meant that the AnyaNya was recognized as an autonomous militant force. To what extent can the formation of the AnyaNya Forces be attributed to SANU leadership? Did SANU practically control the AnyaNya Force activities? And to what extent can AnyaNya be considered a military wing of SANU? Answers to such questions varied among SANU leaders, depended on how close each of them was to the AnyaNya military leadership at the time.

For example, George Kwanai and Joseph Oduho, both leading figures of SANU, contended that the decision to form Anya Nya was taken by the SANU executive committee in February 1963. Thus, the Anya Nya was a military wing of SANU, and received its orders from it. At the other extreme, William Deng Nhial, who was SANU Secretary General, argued that the Anya Nya had formed itself into a military force and it was later on that they approached SANU for endorsement.[4]

Whatever the truth may be, several indications had revealed that SANU leadership tried hard to build the Anya Nya up into an effective military arm of the political leadership in exile. The decision to opt for war' seemed to have been taken when the politicians in exile became convinced that the use of force had become the only alternative to a peaceful dialogue. However, it is worth emphasing here that the SANU's leadership had not officially associated itself with the Anya Nya military activities despite the fact of its assistance.[5]

The name 'AnyaNya'

Historians and former AnyaNya leaders differ as to the origins and the meaning of the name 'AnyaNya'. Some said it comes from the Madi language, which means 'Snake Venom'. Oliver Albino translates it literally to mean 'venom of the Gabon viper' in Madi, Moru and Lotuko languages. Edgar O'Balance simply called it 'snake poison'. Cecil Eprile traced it to an old legend said to be Lotuko version of the term 'Inyanya' which in the Madi and Moru languages, means literally 'the venom of the Gabon viper'.[6]

Whatever is the true origin of the term, it was adopted in the mid of 1963. Other names such as 'Freedom fighters', 'People of Forests' or 'People of Bushes' and many more other local names were used by the local inhabitants. It is to be noted that at the beginning of the movement, the name 'AnyaNya' was used for both military and the political wings of the movement, but later on it was exclusively used for the military forces.

The Rise and the Development of the Anyanya Movement

Recruitment

In any guerrilla movement recruitment in itself is not important nor are the number of the training centers; rather, it is the number and the types of recruits that matter. In the AnyaNya movement the recruitment process was confined to each locality and carried out in accordance with the conditions of each region. In its early stages, the AnyaNya recruits came from four types of groups:[7]
1. The mutineers of the Torit garrison of August 18th, 1955 who went into hiding in the Southern Sudan bushes, and those who went to exile in the neighbouring countries
2. Those who, due to personal problems, such as court conviction, imprisonment, or those who escaped from service and decided to join the movement.
3. Those who fled from Juba and Wau in July 1965 following the massacres in these towns.
4. Government spies who took opportunity to join the ranks of the movement with the aim of reporting back to the government.

The process of recruitment in the three Southern provinces underwent different phases.

Equatoria Province

In Equatoria province, especially in the western part of the province, the recruitment process was made easy by the availability of fighters and former servicemen who fled the town after the mutiny of 1955.

The new recruits were first trained at the local camps then sent to Zaire (DRC) for more intensified training. The man in charge of the preliminary training in the region at that time was certain captain Marko Bangusa. By the beginning of 1965 there were already about a thousand trained fighters ready to fight in the province. Some of the trained fighters were assigned the task of collecting guns from the civilians either by rewarding them or by forcing those owners who refused to give their weapons. All types of guns were collected: muzzle-leaders, magnum rifles, few British rifles, Remingtons and short guns. The recruits were also asked to bring with them their arrows, bows, spears, knives and swords.[8]

In August 1964, two-inch mortars, machine guns, and grenades were either captured or bought from 'Simba' Congolese guerrilla by the AnyaNya in the Equatoria province.

Bahr El Ghazal Province

The first transit training camp in Bahr El Ghazal was established in 1964 at Ngo Suluge. Having completed their local training recruits were sent to Zaire, (DRC) for more training. Those areas which had no access to reach Zaire, Duim Zubeir, Raga and surrounding areas had their recruits trained in the (Central Africa Empire) the current Central African Republic, near border town of Mboki.[9]

Like in Equatoria, arms were collected from the local population. In November 1963, for example, a certain Ferdinand Chol, captured two rifles from police at Bussere village. British rifles were captured in Khor Ghaba village by a band of AnyaNya, which attacked a police station. In August 1964, six automatic rifles were collected by a brave young woman from policemen whom she induced to her house. In December 1964 an AnyaNya force attacked

Bingi village where it captured many arms.

It is worth mentioning that muzzle-loaders were possible to load one gun with (60) to (80) lead balls. A single shot of such size if fired at a group of the government forces it could injure all and kill many. As such it was called by the AnyaNya in Arabic 'Kulu Kum' literally means 'all of you'.[10]

Upper Nile Province

The guerrilla organization process in Upper Nile Province began as early as 1960. By June 1962 the official process of recruitment and training began. One of the organizers of the AnyaNya movement in Upper Nile, Commander Daniel Nyang Rundial summarized the establishment of the organization as follows:

> The period before 1960 was characterized by a general threat to one's self, people were arrested and jailed without trial including students. The policy of government did very much to encourage the mass exodus of Southerners from towns to bush and hence to the neighbouring countries. I was among those who took refuge in Ethiopia and remained there in asylum in a refugee camp with no idea of organizing fighting forces against the Northerners. It was in 1960 that Philip Pedak Lieth left his studies in Britain came to Ethiopia and wrote to me asking me and others to organize a fighting Force in Upper Nile in October 1961. As an ex-policeman with military knowledge, I accepted the offer and started my work. I started the movement (AnyaNya forces) in Upper Nile, saw its development ends in 1972.[11]

REVOLUTION ON EQUATORIA MOUNTAINS

After his arrival from England, Philip Pedak organized in July 1962 a conference in one of the biggest refugee camps on the Ethiopian-Sudan border, and it was agreed that Commander Daniel Nyang Rundial be assigned the responsibility for military organization and training of the AnyaNya. By July 10th, 1963 about one hundred trained men were under command of Daniel Nyang. For the time being the military base was established in Adelin camp near Sudan-Ethiopian border.[12] Unlike in the other two other provinces the AnyaNya forces in Upper Nile province at its initial stage came from Nuer community. In fact, the one hundred men who initiated the AnyaNya in the province were all for Nuers. Later on ten Anuak tribesmen led by Paul Oter and Paul Nyegore joined the movement. In September 1963, Shiluk, Dinka, Murle and others joined the AnyaNya in a large numbers at the provincial level.

In fact in October 1963, in the whole of the Upper Nile province there were only three Magnum rifles. The main supplier of arms to the AnyaNya was the enemy. The first major operation against the army occurred on December 16th, 1963 at Pochalla police post in Boma Plateau. The attack was commanded by Daniel Nyang and five men. As a result, two rifles were collected. Earlier they managed to collect thirty magnum guns from Chief Koarlo Kusi, the Murle chief.[13]

On December 28th, a second attack on Pochalla was launched by the AnyaNya, in which the government armed forces in the post were surprised and an automatic rifle and about 6000 rounds were captured. The attackers reported to have lost one fighter that they considered a big lost at the very time they were disparately in need of manpower.

The Rise and the Development of the Anyanya Movement

The effectiveness of the first two attacks on Pochalla and in the success was enormous. Civilians began to join the AnyaNya voluntarily, thus, the recruitment figures rose from about (180) to about a thousand by January 1964. The civilians, having realized the seriousness and capabilities of the AnyaNya forces, began to give in their private guns that numbered to about (60) magnum rifles by the middle of 1964.

By the mid of 1965 the recruitment in the three Southern provinces has been well organized. Each region had its own central camp to which the recruits were sent. It was also decided that, for disciplinary purposes, a procedure of selection had to be devised. Thus before a recruit was accepted to become a member of the force, she or he had to take an allegiance oath, which was administered by a regimental sergeant of the central camp. The recruit was asked to answer the following questions:[14]

- Why did she or he decide to join the movement
- Would she/he be ready to suffer without food, clothing, medical cares and undergoes all sorts of hardships, which might lead to the lost of her/his life. For a man recruit he was asked to keep away from women and abide by the laws of the movement.
- She/he must be committed and loyal to the movement to the last.
- Must not betray or work against the movement.
- Must do everything to destroy all the enemies of the movement even if that enemy is his/her own relative.

Once the new recruit had answered in affirmative the above questions, a Bible was placed in proper place, a spear, a gun and bullets were place together. Then the oath taker put his right hand on them and repeated the following words after the oath administrator:

"I ----- (name) ----- promise in the name of almighty God and those present to work honestly for the defense of my country, Southern Sudan, and that I will execute the orders of my commanders as may be passed onto me and will accept any punishment levied on me should I be found guilty as a result of disobedience.[15]

The oath taking in the movement had two purposes: to secure military obedience and to see to it that the new recruit has voluntarily accepted to serve his country. In 1963 an AnyaNya emblem was created. It composed of a buffalo surrounded by two snakes, the whole split by an arrow, which symbolized the buffalo bull's might, the deadliness of a snake and the accuracy of the arrow.[16]

From the above discussion it could be observed that at its initial stages the Anyanya obtained its recruits through voluntary and spontaneous response of Southerners to join the movement. Secondly weaponry was obtained either through donation of civilians or through first operations against the government army. Moreover, these operations for the movement, the supplies such as: food, money, medical care and all the expenses for opening up of bush schools were obtained from the local population. Finally, at initial stage, there was no foreign element, mercenary or otherwise, that participated in the training of the fighters. In fact, the neighbouring countries were not against the movement, but at the same time they did not support it financially or militarily. However, they allowed the movement to use their territories for training purposes. In addition, they welcomed hundreds of thousands of Southern Sudanese in their countries as civilian refugees. They even facilitated education for the Southern Sudanese students and admitted them to the government schools at all levels. [17]

The Propaganda

The popular and political mobilization in the Anyanya went in two parallel ways: the one carried out by the SANU in exile through published magazines abroad. On the other hand, the internal propaganda was carried out in the "liberated" areas by a special unit called "political agents". The objective of the second type of propaganda was to mobilize Southern Sudanese masses and to explain to them the objectives of the movement. The AnyaNay's propagandists concentrated on three points that appealed directly to the Southern masses: [18]

- That the government army in the South was an army of occupation.
- That this army was not only at war with the AnyaNya but mainly with all the people of the South. The evidence was the harsh treatment and the burning of villages, murdering of women, children and the aged by the government forces.
- That the Northerners do not care about Southern Sudanese people but only interested in obtaining the fertile land of the South. The North was accused of collected taxes from Southerners to develop the North.

The 'political agent's' propaganda went like this:
'Are you ready to donate money to the Arabs to buy arms to come and shoot you with? Or to whom do you think you can give your money – to us or to the Arabs?'[19]

Through well-articulated propaganda the AnyaNya won popular support and as a result more recruits joined the movement.

The Organizational Structure of the AnyaNya Movement

After the formation of the Southern Sudan Provisional Government, SSPG in August 1967, it was decided that the military wing of the movement, the AnyaNya, should be reorganized both at provincial and regional levels. The military structure of the AnyaNya was divided into Home Guards, Territorial Forces and the Mobile Forces.

The Territorial Forces

The recruits who composed this force were mainly from local villages. They were influential in mobilizing and convincing the local population of the objectives of the movement. Their number depended on the environment and the density of the population inhabiting a particular area. Their function was to protect the local population from government army attacks. Their military tactics ranged from breaking bridges to ambushes.[21]

The AnyaNya Military Structure

Organization of an Independent Regional Force (Figure A)

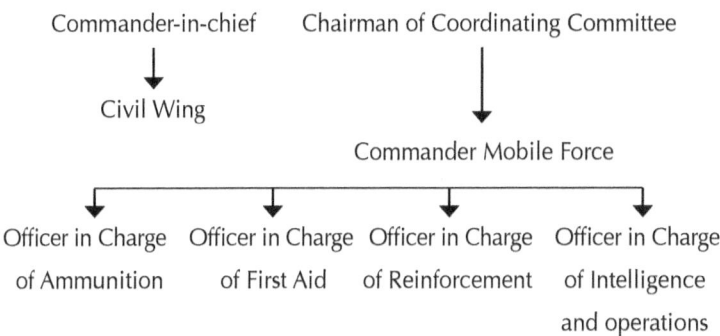

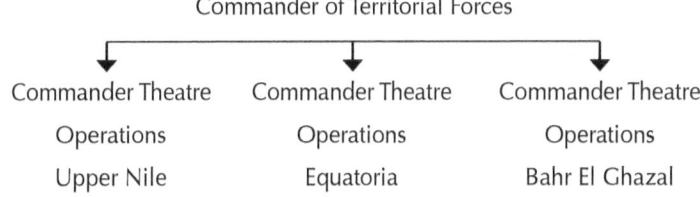

The Mobile Forces or National Force

This force composed of Combined Territorial Forces from different regions. Commanded by senior officer of coordinating committee, they were well armed and mobilized and had no specific base, but in constant alert to reinforce and to relief those forces overcome by the government troops. Their theatres of operations were police posts and army garrisons throughout the South. [22] (Refer to Figure A).

Unlike most of the guerrilla Forces in Africa at the time, the AnyaNya Forces from initial stages had stationed its camps near the internal borders within the Southern Sudan. The major camps were situated deep in the forests where enemy access was near to impossible. Thus, in case of a defeat the transfer of the camp could be manageable and it was easy to step over the border. Moreover the food supply and the density of the population were important in terms of the number of camps and the fighters in particular areas. [23]

In fact, the AnyaNya made it a point not to exhaust the resources of a particular area in order to avoid the starvation of the local population. Indeed, the number of weapons also determined the location and the number of the camps. In other words, the headquarters needed most the highest number of staff and fighters; their work consisted of day-to-day activities, reserve for reinforcement; personnel for communication between camps, since there were no cars or tracks, or radios for communication. Guards for documents and ammunitions were also needed; not to mention guards for stores of supply. [24]

Sources of Weaponry

Up to 1964 the AnyaNya Forces depended solely on the government army for their weapons. All types of arms were captured: American, Belgian, Chinese, Britain and Russian. However, none of these countries backed the AnyaNya. According to Wakoson, a political officer in the movement, the AnyaNya obtained their first huge number of arms when the Sudan government allowed the delivery of arms to the Congolese 'Simba' guerrilla through Southern Sudan. These arms were supplied by Egypt, China and Algeria. In fact, in 1965:

The Rise and the Development of the Anyanya Movement

The AnyaNya intercepted a convey between Yei and Zairian border. The AnyaNya captured the arms and ammunitions. This was the largest arms gain the movement ever got. Following the Congolese Simba defeat and their influx into Sudan, they exchanged their weapons for food, clothes and sometimes mercenaries bartered these arms for Leopard skins, elephant tasks ... At one point a certain captain Peter believed to be an American was deeply involved in this trade..."[25]

The second source of AnyaNya arms was from government regular army. Some Sudanese army officers sold secretly their guns and ammunitions to the AnyaNya local commanders. This was true as far as German made GIM3 and the Belgian FN gun were concerned. Both guns used the same bullets, twenty each. The exchange of arms between the local commanders was purely business like in nature.[26]

The third, but the main source of the AnyaNya arms, came from Israel in July 1969. According to the government reports West Germany, Americans and especially Israel were supplying the AnyaNya with arms, however, the AnyaNya denied any involvement of Germans or Americans because:

The only country in the world known to have openly given military aid to the Southern Sudan Liberation Movement was Israel. The Israeli aid to the South did not have moral or ideological grounds. It actually meant stabling the Arabs- including Northern Sudanese who deemed to be fighting for Arab cause in the South in the back.[27]

The AnyaNya commanders admitted that they saw Israeli officers in Southern Sudan in July 1969, where equipment were dropped by Israeli planes into AnyaNya guerrilla areas via Ethiopia and Uganda.

The Anya Nya organizational structure civil administration

The organizational structure of the proposed administration was similar all over the South with slight differences in some areas. The AnyaNya government organizational structure was as follows:

Home Guards or Village Scouts

This group composed of young villagers, who for security reasons were kept secret. They were trained in asuch way that they should know the political philosophy of the movement in all its aspects. While they were not armed, their leaders were armed with pistols and grenades. They were ordinary citizens living in their own houses. It was difficult for a new comer to the village to identify them from ordinary villagers.[28] Their work was to caution the civilians of any government forces attack. They used whistles, horns, wood pipe, drums etc. All the inhabitants were aware of each instrument's special code, which transmitted messages of danger or an assembly for a special occasion. They coordinated their work with village committees and political agents. They coordinated relationship between villages and the AnyaNya authorities. For administrative purposes, the AnyaNya received their military orders from local commanders and their civilian instructions came from each village committee. They were efficient in identifying and arresting spies, who came from towns claiming to be visiting their relatives in the villages.[29]

Village Committees

These committees normally composed of five to ten members. Being the elders of each community, their work was to collect taxes from population. Each person was asked to pay 50 piasters or two Sudanese pounds. The taxation system depended on the wealth of each region. In addition to civil powers, they were vested with a judicial authority through local courts created to solve civil cases such as rape, feuds among clans, theft and adultery. In these courts, customary law was the source of judgments. Those cases connected with political, criminal and security of the region were sent to the AnyaNya headquarters.[30]

Recruitment Centres

As mentioned earlier, the preliminary training was administered by a senior officer sent from the regional camp. He was assisted by a civilian who was normally a resident of the village where the centre was situated. The initial training was where indoctrination and capabilities of a recruit were tested. The recruit was sent to the central camp for further intensified training.

Political Agents

These were students who joined the movement, they were appointed by the president in the headquarters. Their assignment was to enlighten the village committees about the objectives and the activities of the movement. They were often available to console the villagers in time of hardships.

Executive Officer

He was empowered with judicial authority and cooperated with political agents. His function was to manage finances and the supplies of the movement. He was assisted by civil administrators. His superior was the District Commissioner. He represented the civil administration unit in the movement.[31]

District Commissioner DC

He was vested with political, administrative and judicial powers in his district. In every district the DC was assisted by three to four assistants, including a senior police officer. The later assignment was to help the DC in investigation of criminal cases. All District Commissioners in the AnyaNya liberated areas were subordinates to the coordinating committee the highest body of civil administration.

The Coordinating Committee

This committee was headed by a Chairman and a Secretary General. The committee was the "shadow cabinet" of the AnyaNya. It composed of secretaries of administration, finance, political affairs and defense and security. The Chairman of the committee resided in the military headquarters, somewhere in the South. Other departments such as agriculture, health, education, information and culture were vested in the President who may, if need arises, assign them to individuals, through elections. Any post left vacant for whatever reason was filled by election. This procedure continued in the movement until General Joseph Lagu took over the leadership of the AnyaNya in July 1970.[32]

The AnyaNya Military and Civilian Organization

Civilian Wing	Military Wing
Provincial Commissioners	Regional Commanding Officers
District Commissioners	Theatres of Operations
Sub-District Commissioners	Commanders of Mobile Forces

Heads of Various Departments

Village Police & Scouts

Political Agents

Village Committees

Civilians in the AnyaNya liberated areas

Joint Civilian and Military Board (Province Council)

All the members of this Board were drawn from members of the Coordinating Committee. It coordinated the military operations at the regional level and distributed arms to the units. It planned, reviewed military strategies and settled problems between zone commanders. The Board was the supreme authority over all military issues in the AnyaNya movement.

From the above description of the AnyaNya military and administrative organization, one would get the impression that the AnyaNya was an efficient organization, capable of meeting the needs of the local population. Although this was the case to some extent, the AnyaNya had its own administrative and political weaknesses. These included lack of educated elite; personal misuse of movement funds; poverty, shortage of external sources of supply, high death rate from diseases; nonexistence of communications and transport, lack of knowledge of the techniques used by other guerrilla movements; and above all, the handicaps of ethnicity and internal differences. However, there existed also sources of strengths in the AnyaNya: The courage and resourcefulness of the resistance fighters, i.e. their sense of dedication to the cause of their resistance.[33]

AnyaNya's Liabilities

Among other things, the Anya Nya had at the beginnings the following visible liabilities:
- Lack of discipline,
- Poor structural organization;

- Little combat experience,
- Inferior military equipment,*
- Shortage of external assistant,
- Smallness of the educated personnel;
- Lack of support from neighbouring African countries
- Limited knowledge of guerrilla warfare techniques
- High death rate from disease, which affected both the Anya Nya and the local population.
- Tribalism and sectional differences, which often led to inter-factional fights in the movement.[34]

The Birth of the Southern Sudan Liberation Movement (SSLM)

It is true that there was direct link between the emergence of political organizations in Southern Sudan and the development of the AnyaNya into a national liberation movement, both of which help in the consolidation of the Southern Sudanese political direction. Of course it is difficult to attribute the rise of Southern political work to a particular group of politicians.61. Perhaps where political awareness had solid base was in the Anya Nya movement. Indeed, with a solid popular support behind it, the Anya Nya had by September 1969, found itself faced with the challenge and the task of uniting Southern Sudanese political and military leaders. The Anya Nya was therefore, the only political group qualified to play the role of unifier. Unlike other Southern politicians who spent most of their time in East Africa, the Anya Nya leadership lived among the local population in villages and in the refugee camps.³⁵

In order to achieve unity among the Southern Sudanese leadership in exile, Colonel Joseph Lagu, then the Anya Nya commander of Eastern Equatoria region, began a very complex and difficult task of uniting, first the Anya Nya forces, and then the Southern politicians under his leadership. Lagu himself admitted the difficulties he encountered while trying to unite the Southern resistance movement:

> The most difficult thing (sic) I faced in the bush was how to deal with the politicians. I just (sic) refused to cooperate with them...The fighters saw that my work was better and so they deserted the politicians.³⁶

In October 1969, having received allegiance of the most senior Anya Nya officers in the three Southern Provinces, Lagu formed the Anya Nya High Command Council. The task of this Council, he hoped, would be to control and direct the military operations and to acquire military equipment.* In addition to this, the council would administer the civilian population in areas under the Anya Nya control.³⁷ Colonel Lagu was aware that his immediate opponents were the politicians who had attempted, but failed, to gain effective control of the Anya Nya.

Colonel Lagu began his difficult mission by dissolving various self-proclaimed governments using senior Anya Nya officers to achieve this end. In April 1970, Colonel Lagu managed to persuade General Emedio Taffeng to dissolve his Anyidi Revolutionary

Government and joined him along with other senior officers. Next, Colonel Lagu engineered a coup against Nile Provincial Government by winning over the NPG's Chief of Staff, Colonel Fredrick Magott and appointed him Commander of the Western Equatoria region. Convinced by his success in winning over supporters among Southern Sudanese intellectuals, masses and students, Lagu called for a conference in August 1971 in which Southern military and political leaders came together.[38] The conference marked the Sixteenth Anniversary of the Torit mutiny of August 1955.

The conference, held at "Owiny Ki-Bul"* resolved the formation of the 'Southern Sudan Liberation Movement, SSLM'. The 'AnyaNya National High Command Council' was also confirmed. Perhaps the most significant resolution of the conference was that all the Southern politicians, without exception, had dissolved their 'Governments' and movements and unanimously approved Lagu's leadership. Joseph Lagu promoted himself to Major General. Despite General Lagu's attempts to campaign for African and international recognition of the SSLM, his efforts had failed totally. The 'Governing Authority' as General Lagu preferred to call his command was approved and formed as follows:

High Command
Major General Joseph Lagu Yanga, C-In-C
Brigadier Joseph Akuon, Commander 2nd Brigade, Upper Nile
Col. Fredrick Magott, Commander 1st Brigade, Equatoria
Col. Emmanuel Abur, Senior Officer, 3rd Brigade, Bahr El Ghazal.[39]

High Civil Authority
Elia Lupe, Chief Commissioner
Elisapana Mulla, Commissioner of Equatoria.
Antipas Ayiei, Commissioner for Upper Nile
Dishan Ojwe, Police Commissioner.

There was no commissioner appointed for Bahr Al Ghazal province until the Addis Ababa Agreement, February 1972.[40]

Emissaries
Mading Garang - London
Lawrence Wol Wol - Paris
Dominic Mohammed - Washington
Angelo Vogu - East Africa (Kampala, Uganda)
Job Adier - Addis Ababa.[41]

By September 1971, it was estimated that the Anya Nya strength was between 5,000 and 40,000 men. The Anya Nya sources put the number at 12,000 full timers with thousands more part timers or reserves.[42]

With Lagu's ascendancy to the top of Southern Sudan Liberation Movement, there seemed to have been enough Southern support behind him to make peace with General Jaafar Nimeiri.* In fact, by December 1971, it had become clear to all sides of the Sudanese conflict that neither political integration by force, nor secession by insurrection was a genuine a feasible solution to the Southern problem. Having acknowledged this reality, the two sides of the conflict accepted and invited the World Council of Churches, and

The Rise and the Development of the Anyanya Movement

the All-African Conference of Churches and Anglican Churches to mediate a peaceful settlement.[43] The mediators' mission was to find a settlement within the framework of a united Sudan. The World Council of Churches and All-African Conference of Churches had helped in many ways. They provided the SSLM leaders with financial support for fares, accommodation, administrative services when attending conferences, and for legal and constitutional advice in person of Mr. Dingle Foot. Indeed, between the signature of the Addis Ababa Agreement on 27th February 1972, and its ratification by the Southern Sudan Liberation Movement on 28th March, the Anglican Archbishop of Jerusalem and the Superior General of Verona Fathers, both in Uganda at the time, exerted all their influence in favour of its acceptance by the Southern Sudanese.[44]

Neither Federation nor a sovereign independent state in the South was provided for in the Addis Ababa Agreement. The South got instead, the revised version of the March 1965 "Local Autonomy" which the North had proposed to the Southern delegates to the Round Table Conference. It was a compromise which could not have materialized unless Northern as well as Southern politicians and military leaders had realized that peaceful and open dialogue was the sole guarantor for any lasting peace in the country.[45]

The Addis Ababa peace agreement had finally brought to an end a long period of hostility and military confrontation. It was hoped that the Accord would mark the beginning of a new spirit of cooperation, coordination and free dialogue between the North and the South. Indeed, it was hoped that the Addis Ababa Agreement would erase the "Torit Mutiny Legacy" from the minds of Southern Sudanese.[46]

End Notes

1 Eprile, *War and Peace in the Sudan*, p. 96; see Wakoson, "The Origins and Development of the AnyaNya Movement", p. 130.

2 Keith Kyle, "The Sudan Today," *African Affairs*, 65 (1966), pp. 233-244; O'Ballance, *The Secret War in the Sudan*, pp. 96-100.

3 Peter Woodward, "Nationalism and Opposition in Sudan," *African Affairs*, 80 (1981), pp. 379-388; see *SANU Youth Organizaiton Monthly Bulletin* (Khartoum), No. IV, 1968.

4 Howell, "Political Leadership", pp. 186-197

5 O'Balance, *The Secret War in the Sudan*, p. 59; Keith Kyle, "The Southern Problem of the Sudan" *The World Today* 22 (1966), pp. 512-20.

6 Wakoson, "The origin and the Development of the AnyaNya" p. 137; R.K. Badal, "The Rise and Fall of Separatism in Southern Sudan" *African Affairs* 75 (1976), pp. 463-74.

7 Wakoson, Sam C. Sarkessian, "The Southern Sudan: Reassassment", *African Studies Review* 16 (1973), pp. 1-20.

8 Ibid., pp. 1-20.

9 O'Balance, *The Secret War in the Sudan*, pp. 60-61; Wai, *The African Arab Conflict in the Sudan*, p. 92.

10 Wakoson, "The Origin and the Development of the AnyaNya", p. 140.

11 Ibid., p. 141.

12 John Howell, "The Politics in the Southern Sudan" *African Affairs* 72 (April 1973), pp. 163-178. Wai, *The African-Arab Conflict in the Sudan*, p. 92.

13 Wakoson, "The Origin and Development of the AnyaNya", p. 145.

14 Ibid., p. 146.

15 Cecil, *War and Peace in the Sudan*, p. 97.

16 Kenneth W. Grundes, "Nationalism and Separatism in East Africa" *Africa* (February 1968), pp. 90-94/112.

17 Wakoson, "The Origin and Development of the AnyaNya", pp. 132-135.

18 Ibid., p. 134.

19 Ibid., p. 152.

20 Ibid., p. 152.

21 Ibid., p. 153.

The Rise and the Development of the Anyanya Movement

22 Ibid., p. 158.
23 Peter Woodward, "Nationalism and Opposition in the Sudan" *African Affairs* 80 (1981), pp. 379-388.
24 Cecil, *War and Peace in the Sudan*, p. 96.
25 Wakoson, "The Origin and Development of the AnyaNya", p. 158.
26 Ibid., p. 159.
27 Keith Kyle, "The Sudan Today" *African Affairs* 65 (1966), pp. 233-244.
28 Ibid., pp. 233-240.[57]
29 Praha Blanka Richova, "The Ethnic Conflict as the Factor of State coherence in Africa: The Case of the sudan" *Archive* Orientatalni 59(1991), pp. 289-312.
30 Wakoson, Thomas H. Greene, *Comparative Revolutionary Movements* (NJ: Prentice-Hall, Inc., 1990), pp. 88-103.
31 Wai, *The African-Arab Conflict in the Sudan*, pp. 112-114. Cecil, War and Peace in the Sudan, p. 97.
32 Eprile, *War and Peace in the Sudan*, p. 77-97. *In July 1964 the AnyaNya began to acquire arms. Most of these arms had been originally transported from Egypt and Algeria via Southern Sudan, to Congolese *Simbas* rebels under Christopher Gbanye. Some of the arms were either abandoned or sold to AnyaNya by the *Simbas* following their defeat in October 1965.
33 Howell, "Political Leadership", p. 256.
34 Alier, *Southern Sudan*, p. 68.
35 Howell, "Political Leadership", p. 265. *During General Lagu's leadership the AnyaNya-Israeli relations were strengthened. In fact these relations began as early as August 1967, following the Six Days War between Arabs and the Israelis. Most of the Israelis military aid to AnyaNya were channelled through Ethiopia to the AnyaNya bases in Upper Nile province and Uganda. The Israelis were expelled from Uganda by President Idi Amin on March 24, 1972, the day on which Colonel Lagu left Kampala for final talks on ratification in Addis Ababa.
36 Eprile, *War and Peace in the Sudan*, pp. 98-102.
37 * "*Owiny-Ki Bul*' was another code name for the Southern Sudan Liberation movement's headquarters. It is found in the Imatong mountains in Equatoria province; however, the cape where the C-in-C office was located remained one of the AnyaNya secrets. Details of Lagu's ascendency to power are provided by O'Ballance, *The Secret War in the Sudan*, pp. 135-141.
38 Eprile, *War and Peace in the Sudan*, p. 99.
39 Ibid., p. 99.
40 Ibid., p. 99.

41 *The military coup of Colonel Jaafar Nimeiri, on 25 May 1969, and its aftermath is discussed in details and in length by Alier, *Southern Sudan*, pp. 54-163. Alier was Vice President when he led the government delegation to peace talks with the SSLM. Later on he became President of the "High Executive Council" as the government in the Southern Region became known. The full text of the Addis Ababa Agreement is found in Dustan M. Wai, ed. *The Southern Sudan and the Problem of the National Integration* (London: Frank Cass, Ltd., 1973), pp. 221-244. Also see Timothy C. Niblock, "A New political system in the Sudan", *African Affairs* 73, (October 1974), pp. 408-418.

42 The role of the World Council of Churches, WCC in the Sudanese Peace Talks is traced by Wai, *The African-Arab Conflict in the Sudan*, pp. 142-166.

43 Gabriel R. Warburg, " National identity in the Sudan: Fact, Fiction and Prejudice in ethnic and religious Relations," *Asian and African Studies*, 24 (1990), pp. 151-202; also see Nelson Kasfir. "Southern Sudanese politics since the Addis Ababa Agreement" *African Affairs* 76 (April 1977), pp. 143-166; Sanderson, *Education, Religion and Politics in Southern Sudan*, pp. 431-435.

44 Peter K. Bechtold, "Military Rule in the Sudan: The First Five Years of Ja'far Numayri," *The Middle East Journal*, 29 (1975), pp. 16-32; see also Richard P. Stevens, "The 1972 Addis Ababa Agreement and the Sudan's Afro-Arab Policy," *The Journal of Modern African Studies*, 14, 2 (1976), pp. 247-274; Omer el Haq Musa, "Reconciliation, Rehabilitation and Development Efforts in Southern Sudan," *The Middle East Journal*, (Winter 1973), pp. 1-6.

45 Illustrative details on the October uprising are given by Yusuf Fadl Hasan, "The Sudanese Revolution of October 1964," *The Journal of Modern AFrican Studies*, 5, 4 (1967), pp. 491-509; 46 Henderson, *Sudan Republic*, pp. 203-228; also see David W McClintock, "The Southern Sudan Problem: Evolution of an ARab-African Confrontation," Middle East Journal, 24 (1970), pp. 461-478.

CHAPTER SIX

Conclusion

The outbreak of the Torit mutiny on the Equatoria Mountains has often been considered as the beginning of a new trend in Southern Sudanese politics. However, for several reasons, the mutiny had failed to take a character of a Southern popular uprising: In fact the areas affected by the mutiny and the numbers involved were limited to qualify the Torit revolt as a mass revolution. Yet, it would be wrong at the same time to level it as a simple result of resentment on the part of a frustrated Southern educated class. The revolt had introduced a new regional and ethnic militancy of the Southern communities against the North and that is where lay its revolutionary legacy.[1]

Several factors had contributed to the spread of mutiny and led to its suppression:

The mutiny was concentrated geographically in Equatoria province and the major Nilotic ethnic groups such as Shiluk, Nuer, Anuak and Dinka were not overwhelmingly involved in the mutiny. As a result, the mutiny was not effective in the Upper Nile and Bahr el Ghazal provinces, compared to the situation in Equatoria province. There seemed to have been little region-wide Southern awareness of the political reasons behind the occurrence of the rebellion, at least, during the first week of its outbreak. Again, there was the lack of communication between the three provinces, which made it difficult for the political activists to exchange information regarding the timing of the revolt. The distance was therefore one of the immediate problems that had faced the mutineers.²

There was the lack of organization and coordination between the Southern political leaders and the Equatorial corps, soldiers and public officials in the region. By and large, it seemed that the civilian support for the mutiny came mainly from junior clerks, teachers, police and prison warders. This group composed the Southern intelligensia at the time. It was also this class of people who first took to violence and later formed the nucleus of the Southern resistance movement in early 1960's before the politicians joined them in exile.

Another reason that led to the failure of the mutiny to spread widely was perhaps the British refusal to accept the Egyptian offer for a joint intervention in the South, which gave Prime Minister al-Azhari a free hand to suppress the mutiny militarily.³ However, the Condominium intervention could have incited or perhaps transformed the situation into a general revolution, considering that already in August 1955, rumours of eminent Egyptian invasion of the South, following the British withdrawal, were widely circulated throughout the South. Moreover, the disappearance of the majority of the mutineers from Torit into Southern bushes had disastrous effects to the future peace settlement in the Sudan. In other words, the formation of what later became AnyaNya movement in the South had indeed set off punitive operations by the central government against rebels and these operations, with human loses involved, never ceased until February 1972. Added to this there seemed to have been no specific political objective

Conclusion

that the Equatorial corps' regulars chose to rebel for; they were not acting on their own. Thus the rebellion had created a situation of disillusionment among Southern people, especially among the politicians. Their credibility and ability to provide effective leadership was shaken and became limited.[4]

Few months after the mutiny, visible effects on the Southern political scene were easily traced, especially in three Southern secondary schools and at Khartoum University. Following the suppression of the revolt, all the Southern Secondary schools were transferred to Khartoum due to the insecurity in the region. One of these schools, Rumbek secondary, became the centre of political activity, putting practically Southern parliamentarians under militant pressure. The schools' presence in Khartoum had also helped in promoting relative unity among Southern parliamentarians.

Indeed, school wallpapers such as *candor* and *Spark* reflected what amounted to "a Southern regional viewpoint and a wider Southern political awareness of racial and cultural distinction from the North."[5] The papers went far as talking of "a Northern problem" which arose from failure of the North to face up to the question of identity: "Do we belong to the Middle East or Africa? If to Middle East, then there was no room for the South in such political community; if to Africa, there was great need for a major psychological adjustment on the part of the North".[6] In Northern view however, their affiliation to the Middle East was not opened to question:

> Arab Sudanese looked almost exclusively to Arab culture
> and the Arab world for their political aspirations and

identification. It was natural that they should do so, since undoubtedly they were more Arab than African in their culture. Even nominally Islamicized African tribes with only a veneer of Arab culture, were giving themselves Arab genealogies."[7]

Further radical views were also expressed at Khartoum University where Southern Sudanese students had established newspapers such as *Negro* and *Observer*. These papers, in contrast to their Northern counter-parts, tended to be militant and secessionist in approach. Attacks on 'Northern political domination' and 'Force Islamization and Arabicization' of the South were blatantly expressed. Southern Sudan as a 'potential separate entity' was widely propagated by the students.

The Torit mutiny was considered as the 'beginning of the liberation of the South' and the AnyaNya guerrilla Force was referred to as 'Southern Freedom Fighters', while the pro-government papers at the University simply referred to the AnyaNya as 'mutineers'. The effect of these views on the Southern urban community was of course enormous hormone, considering that those who propagated these views later on became the leading figures in the Southern resistance movement.[8]

With secondary schools and the university students present in Khartoum, Southern politicians and parliamentarians became directly accountable to their constituents, as Southern urban opinion began to take shape in Khartoum. Add to this a considerable number of Southern secondary school students went to military, police and teacher colleges.

Conclusion

Another aspect of the Torit mutiny on the national politics was that it revealed clearly the Northern Sudanese fear of possible Southern secession. The Southern call for federation before Torit mutiny was often associated with separation. Even after the mutiny, Southern exiles spent some time persuading political leaders in the North to give due consideration to Southern demands for equality and participation in the political life of the country. That was why SANU had called for the independence of the South as a last resort, since the ruling elite in the North, both civilian and military, had refused Southern call for a federal union.[9]

Indeed the Northern political parties had consistently blamed General Abboud regime for interrupting the process of constitutional dialogue, which they hoped, would have put an end to the Southern fears and suspicions of Northern domination. The military coup of November 1958 was therefore considered responsible for the emergence of the AnyaNya rebel movement; because had the Southern politicians remained inside the country, and not forced into exile by the military regime, it could have been difficult, if not impossible, for the mutineers to regroup themselves into effective fighting force without political support. The mere presence of political exiles in East Africa had been sufficient enough for the continuity of what became known as 'The Southern problem'.

But again, the existence of exiles was not most of the time in advantage of the 'Southern cause' because of sectarian and ethnic divisions; most of these politicians lacked strong political and social base. Ethnicity for instance, was essential for electoral success in the South. Ironically, most of the politicians, once elected, their ties with the community became weak. Consequently in the years that followed the Torit revolt, the South was to lack both the coherence of leadership and strong effective social bases of politics, which were essential for the development of political organizations. Even the Liberal Party had failed to fill in that role.[10]

Looking at the Torit mutiny in a militant perspective, it had certainly closed the door for appeasement, reconciliation and negotiation between the Southern and Northern politicians. The failure of March 1965 Round Table Conference for example, seemed to have been inevitable considering that the Southern representatives from exile presented uncompromising proposals, most of which were connected with their old suspicions of Northern intentions. After all, most of Southern representatives to the conference were themselves the same parliamentarians of the last parliament that the military regime dissolved. Once the negotiations had started it was difficult for the two parties to change their incompatible goals; thus the chances of resolving the Sudanese conflict were almost non-existence.[11]

Perhaps, the absence of a third party to mediate between them, coupled with a lack of committed and unified leadership of both sides contributed to the failure of the conference. Also the existence of weak coalition governments from 1964 onward became an obstacle toward a negotiated settlement; the Northern parties were preoccupied with their sectarian power struggle more than solving the Southern problem. The army on the other hand was preoccupied with war of attrition against Anya Nya.

Having been just overthrown by a popular uprising in October 1964, the army leadership found itself unable to take any step without politicians' permission. This permission was never granted,

Conclusion

which forced the army, unjustifiably though, to take over from the civilian rule in May 1969.12 The army coup was led by Colonel Jaafar Mohammed Nimeiri, a year later Colonel Joseph Y. Lagu took over and united the Southern Sudan Liberation Movement under his leadership.

It was perhaps then that peace talks between Khartoum and the Southern liberation movement became feasible. The two Sudanese military leaders seemed to have been convinced by the practical difficulties involved in waging guerrilla warfare. They were perhaps more qualified than politicians, to reach a compromise.13 To this effect, President Nimeiri issued a policy statement on the evening of 9th June 1969, in which he said:

"...(T)he revolutionary government is confident and competent enough to face existing realities. It recognizes historical and cultural differences between the North and the South and firmly believes that unity of our country must be built on these objective realities. The Southern people have a right to develop their respective cultures and traditions within a united Sudan."[14]

Consequently Colonel Lagu officially responded by issuing his own policy statement on August 11th, 1971, in which, among other things, he said:

...(A)s far as the Southern Sudanese are concerned, it is well recorded in history that our attitude has always been to find a peaceful solution to the Southern cause. Therefore in conformity with this constant policy for a negotiated settlement that we have pursued during the reign of different and consecutive governments in Khartoum, we call upon General el-Nimeiri to meet the Southern Sudan Liberation Movement to determine conditions aimed at bringing a final end to war and atrocities in South Sudan."[15]

Although there was eventually talk of secession and independence, the Southern Sudan Liberation Movement in 1960's was more focused on Southern problem and less on Sudanese national agenda, which the liberals tried to promote. In fact, the liberals, Southern Front and federalists had fought battles of "constitutional federalism' which had been denied by the Northern politicians since January 1956. The Southern resistance movement was thus concerned with 'regional' recognition. When General Nimeiri recognized the Southern Sudanese people as distinct cultural group, the Anya Nya leadership was ready for a compromise. It was not just 'a regional government' which the South won in February 1972, but an important position within the country's political system which it had never previously held.[16]

The Torit mutiny became a culmination and symbol of 'Southern solidarity'; a symbol of 'rejection of an alien rule' be it British, Egyptians or Northern Sudanese. It was also associated with remembrance of the 'beginning of the struggle for Southern cause' with all its lessons of persecution, sacrifice and heroism.

The August 18th, 1955 became historic day in which Southerners remember the 'Torit martyrs'. The flag of the Equatorial Corps was several times adopted by the Southern Liberation Movements as the "Southern National Flag".[17]

Conclusion

Despite the different interpretations of the causes of the Torit mutiny, its political, social and economic significance among Southern Sudanese, the revolution on the Equatoria Mountains seemed to have developed into a living legend.

End Notes

1. John Howell, "Political leadership and organization in Southern Sudan", pp. 133-156; also see Henderson, *Sudan Republic*, pp. 181-185.
2. Howell, "Political leadership and organization---", pp. 136-150.
3. Ibid., p. 164.
4. Ibid., pp. 133-156.
5. Keith Kyle, "The Southern problem in the Sudan", p. 514.
6. Ibid., pp. 514-520.
7. See Olwadare Agenda. "Arabism and Pan-Arabism in Sudanese Politics". *Journal of Modern African Studies* 11, 2 (1973), pp. 177-200; also see Muddathir Abd al Rahim. "Arabism Africanism and Self-identification in the South". *Sudan in Africa*. ed. Yusuf Fadl Hasan, (Khartoum University Press, 1971), pp. 167-171.
8. Howell, "Political Leadership---", pp. 137-156.
9. Mansour Khalid. *The Government They Deserve: The Role of the Elite in Sudan's Political Evolution*, (London: Kegan Paul International, 1990), pp. 190-192.
10. Howell, "Political leadership---", p. 164.
11. Elias N. Wakoson. "The Origin and Development of the AnyaNya Movement 1955-1972". *Southern Sudan: Regionalism and Religion*. Ed. Mohamed Omer Beshir, (Khartoum University Press, 1984), pp. 127-204.
12. Khalid. *The Government They Deserve*, pp. 162-193.
13. Howell, "Political Leadership", pp. 272-273.
14. Alier, *Southern Sudan*, p. 49.
15. *Grass Curtain*. vol. 212 (October 1971), p. 3.
16. Howell, "Political leadership", pp. 280-283.
17. Ibid., pp. 258-261.

John Gai Yoh holds BA in Political Science and MA in political history from the American University of Beirut (AUB) and PhD in International Politics from University of South Africa in Pretoria. His assignments included Presidential Advisor on Education, Minister of Education, Science & Technology, Head of Government of Southern Sudan (GOSS) Southern African Liaison Office, Pretoria. He also served as South Sudan Ambassador to the Republic of Turkey. Was Resident Research Associate at the Royal Institute for Inter-Faith Studies, Amman, Jordan between July 1996 and May 2003 as well as lecturer at University of South Africa in Pretoria between June 2003-June 2007. He authored several works on Africa, East Africa, Sudan, international politics, conflict management and resolution, regional and international organizations, security and strategic studies.

www.ingramcontent.com/pod-product-compliance
Lightning Source LLC
Chambersburg PA
CBHW032040290426
44110CB00012B/888